ITALIAN COOKING SCHOOL

PASTA

ITALIAN COOKING SCHOOL

PASTA

THE SILVER SPOON KITCHEN

BACK TO BASICS

People often have a preconceived idea that making homemade pasta is an intimidating process and requires highly developed and sophisticated cooking knowledge. On the contrary, pasta is deceptively easy to make and only requires a few basic ingredients. And perhaps just as importantly, the technique is incredibly forgiving where unexpected irregularities in size and shape often lend a rustic charm, without any compromise on taste. This might explain why pasta is one of our favorite comfort foods.

Every pasta shape lends itself to a particular sauce or filling. Whether it's Pappardelle with Mushrooms (see page 24) or a classic Lasagne with Meat Sauce (see page 75) or Duck Ravioli (see page 151), delicious dishes can be prepared once you've mastered the basics and the flavor combinations you'll create are limited only to your imagination.

Italian Cooking School Pasta is easy to navigate and begins with a guide to the basics: pasta types, ingredients, equipment, and a recipe for Fresh Egg Pasta (see page 17). This is followed by chapters on popular pastas— lasagne, tagliatelle, cannelloni, ravioli, and tortellini— and includes recipes that are designed to inspire and tantalize your taste buds.

The joy of making pasta is in the experience of the process, and we encourage you to try your hand on a few of the recipes from each chapter. We also understand the juggling act and busy schedules inherent in modern life—it can be a challenge to make homemade pasta after a long workday, so many of the pasta recipes, particularly in the tagliatelle (see pages 18-69) and lasagne chapters (see pages 70-97), can be substituted with fresh, store-bought pastas. No matter which recipe you choose, you'll bring the flavors of Italy to your home.

FLOUR	Flour is prepared by grinding wheat grains (white flour), which are repeatedly crushed and sifted. Italian flour is classified according to the refining process and labeled as "oo" (the finest), "o," "1," and whole wheat (wholemeal). Flours with high gluten content are particularly well suited to making fresh pasta, and when making egg pasta, "oo," "o," or all-purpose (plain) flour can be used. Look for Italian flours in specialty Italian gourmet stores or online. Other specialty flours include buckwheat flour, whole wheat flour, which is high in fiber and mineral salts, and sweet chestnut flour. When using cup measurements to measure flour, be sure to mix and fluff the flour before measuring. Regardless of how you measure it, sift it afterward before using.
EGGS	Very fresh, top-quality extra-large eggs should be used in the preparation of fresh pasta. Allow a generous ¾ cup (3½ oz/100 g) flour for each egg used. When green pastas are made with vegetables such as spinach, fewer eggs are used because of the vegetables' high water content (on average, one in three eggs is omitted). In some regional recipes, only egg yolks are used, making the pasta more tender and flavorsome.
OIL	Only a very small quantity of extra virgin olive oil is needed—a tablespoon or a little more—in order to make a dough more elastic.

WATER

Very small quantities of lukewarm water can be added to the dough to make it easier to knead and to hydrate the starch in the flour. And, of course, freshly made pasta is cooked in plenty of boiling salted water.

PORTION SIZE

In Italy, pasta is commonly served as a primi, or first course. The portion sizes in this book are designed for main courses and we have allowed about 4 oz/120 g of pasta per person. Most of these recipes can be easily adapted to accommodate more or less servings.

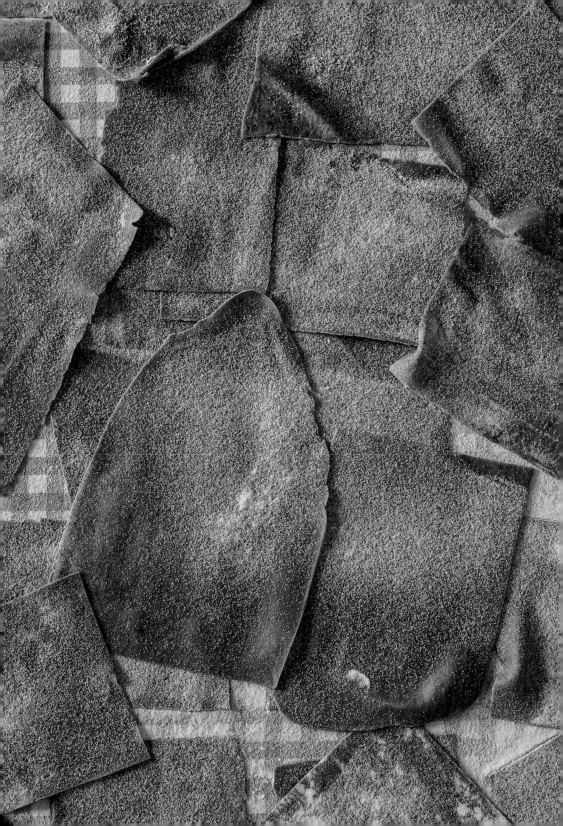

EQUIPMENT

MIXERS	Ingredients can be mixed in a food processor with a kneading attachment. Simply put all the ingredients into the bowl, lower the kneading hook, select the time and speed setting (preferably low), and the pasta dough is ready. Some sophisticated domestic models have cutters to cut the pasta dough into the required shape. By changing accessories and applications, the pasta dough mixer and kneader can also be used for making breads, pizza, etc.
PLASTIC WRAP	Once the pasta dough has been made, it should rest for at least an hour while wrapped in plastic wrap (clingfilm) or covered with a damp dish towel to prevent its drying out.
SPATULA	If mixing the dough by hand, a spatula is useful for gathering up all the dough mixture that remains on the pastry board or work surface during kneading.
PASTA UTENSILS	The pastry wheel is great for cutting out certain pasta shapes—such as pappardelle or maltagliati—evenly, precisely, and swiftly. Pastry cutters enable you to cut out pasta with smooth or ridged edges in a variety of shapes, such as ravioli, tortelli, tortellini, and so on. Finally, use a pastry (piping) bag or teaspoon to fill pastas, such as ravioli.
ROLLING PIN	Made of wood, or other material such as silicone, a rolling pin is indispensable for flattening out the dough before transferring it to an electric or manual pasta machine.

An electric or manual pasta machine has two purposes: to stretch the pasta dough and to cut it into the required shape. In its simplest form, the machine is attached to the table with a clamp. The pasta dough is divided into 5-oz/150-g pieces, then rolled out to a maximum width of ⅜–¾ inch/1–2 cm. Position the rollers at the machine's widest setting, fold the dough in two, and put it through the machine once again. Reduce the gap between the rollers by a couple of notches and repeat the process until you reach the required thickness.

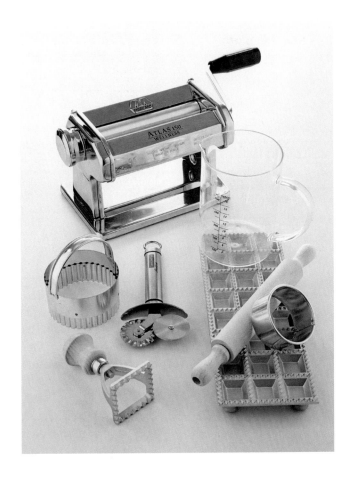

TYPES OF PASTA

TAGLIATELLE

The popular tagliatelle are ribbon pastas (long pasta) that are traditionally cut to a width of ⅜ inch/8 mm and make an ideal pasta for the classic Bolognese meat sauce. Other common ribbon pastas include fettuccine, which are slightly wider (½ inch/1 cm) and thicker (¹⁄₁₆ inch/2 mm) than tagliatelle; pappardelle, which are 2–4-inch/5–10-cm strips with a smooth or ridged border; and taglioni, which are very narrow, almost flat tagliatelle.

LASAGNE

Layered pasta dishes, such as lasagne, are made by cutting the pasta dough into rectangles and overlapping them in several layers and usually accompanied by a tomato and/or béchamel sauce and topped with cheese. Believed to be one of the earliest types of pasta, lasagne is wonderfully versatile and ideal for serving large groups.

CANNELLONI

Cannelloni is a type of stuffed pasta, where rectangular pieces of pasta (4–5 x 3–5-inch/10–12 x 8–12-cm) are dressed with sauce and rolled up around a filling. Popular fillings include spinach and ricotta (see page 101) or ground beef (see page 110).

RAVIOLI

Filled pasta, such as ravioli, are usually stuffed with meat, fish, vegetables, or cheese and served with a sauce that complements the flavor of the filling. Ravioli are squares or half-moon shapes with a meat or cheese and vegetable filling. They are originally from Lombardy but can be found in almost all Italian regions. A similar shape known as tortelli (or tordelli in local dialect) is typical of Lucca, Versilia, and Garfagnana. This semicircular pasta often contains a meat and herb filling. Agnolotti are plump ravioli-like pasta shapes with a meat filling and typical of the Piedmont region.

TORTELLINI

Tortellini are small squares of pasta, folded over a filling, then sealed and pinched together to form a ring. Tortelloni are larger than tortellini and usually filled with spinach and ricotta. Similar pasta in this family include anolini, which are similar to tortellini in shape and traditionally filled with braised beef; cappelletti are triangular pastas shaped like a medieval hat and made with a slightly thicker pasta sheet and a meat filling.

STEP 1

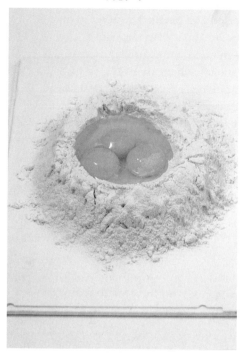

STEP 2

STEP 3

STEP 4

FRESH EGG
PASTA

- Preparation time: *20 minutes
  + 30 minutes resting*
- Calories: *368 cal per
  3½ oz/100 g*
- Makes *1 lb 2 oz/500 g*

INGREDIENTS

- 2⅓ cups (11 oz/300 g) "oo"
  flour
- 3 eggs
- ½ teaspoon olive oil

STEP 1

Sift the flour into a large bowl or a mound on a pastry board, make a well, and break the eggs into it, beating them with a fork. Add the oil and ½ teaspoon of water.

STEP 2

Work in the flour, starting with the inner surfaces of the well. When the eggs and flour start to form a soft dough, work the mixture with your hands to make a ball. Knead for 5 minutes or until smooth and elastic. Wrap in plastic wrap (clingfilm) and rest for 30 minutes.

STEP 3

To roll by machine, cut the rested dough into four. Press each piece into an oblong about 4 x 2 inches/10 x 5 cm. With the rollers at the widest setting, feed the pasta into the machine. Repeat, gradually reducing space between the rollers, until the pasta is the required thinness.

STEP 4

You can also roll out the pasta dough using a rolling pin. Place a ball of dough on a lightly floured work surface and roll it out, turning the circle of dough 45 degrees after each rolling until you have a thin, uniform disk. You can now cut the sheet of pasta dough into the desired shape.

Tip: Flour is always sifted in order to get rid of any lumps and to make it softer and more aerated.

TAGLIATELLE

STEP 1

STEP 2

STEP 3

STEP 4

TECHNIQUE

A LESSON IN TAGLIATELLE

EASY

– Preparation time: *20 minutes*
+ *20 minutes resting*
– *Serves 4*

INGREDIENTS

– 1 quantity Fresh Egg Pasta
  (see page 17)
– flour and fine semolina,
  for sprinkling

STEP 1

Roll out the pasta dough using a pasta machine until
it is approximately ¹⁄₁₆ inch/1 mm thick. Sprinkle
with a little flour or semolina, and dry for 20 minutes,
either hung up on a rack or spread over dry dish cloths.
Dust again with flour or semolina, then roll up
the sheets loosely.

STEP 2

Slice the rolls of pasta to the following thickness,
using a sharp knife: tagliolini (⅛ inch/2–3 mm), taglierini
(⅛ inch/3 mm), fettuccine (¼ inch/5 mm), tagliatelle
(⅜–¼ inch/5–7 mm), or pappardelle (⅜–½ inch/1–1.5 cm).

STEP 3

Once you have cut the pasta into strips, coax them
into the shape of a nest.

STEP 4

Whichever shape you choose to make, transfer the cut
pasta to a tray dusted with semolina. This is coarser
than flour and prevents the pasta from sticking together.
The pasta can be cooked now, covered with a just-damp
cloth to cook later, frozen, or dried completely, ready
to store in airtight containers. For drying, turn the pasta
every now and again so it's evenly exposed to the air.
Pasta can also be cut to form small diamond shapes,
such as maltagliati, seen here.

PAPPARDELLE AL RAGÙ MISTO
PAPPARDELLE WITH MEAT SAUCE

AVERAGE

– Preparation time: *10 minutes*
– Cooking time: *45 minutes*
– Calories per serving: *640*
– *Serves 2*

INGREDIENTS

– 2 tablespoons oil
– 2 tablespoons (1 oz/30 g)
  butter
– ½ onion, finely chopped
– ½ carrot, finely chopped
– 1 stick celery, finely chopped
– 1 oz/30 g bacon, finely
  chopped
– 7 oz/200 g ground (minced)
  beef or pork
– pinch of freshly grated
  nutmeg
– scant ½ cup (3½ fl oz/
  100 ml) red wine
– generous 1 cup (9 oz/250 g)
  canned tomatoes
– 3½ oz/100 g chicken giblets,
  chopped
– ½ quantity fresh
  Pappardelle (see page 21)
– 2–3 tablespoons grated
  Parmesan cheese
– salt and pepper

Heat the oil and half the butter in a skillet or frying pan, add the onion, carrot, celery, and bacon, and cook gently for 10 minutes. Stir, add the beef or pork, and season with salt and pepper and a pinch of grated nutmeg. Cover and cook over low heat for 15 minutes. If it needs moistening, add a little hot water.

When the meat has browned lightly, add the wine, simmer to let it evaporate, and then add the tomatoes. Cover and cook over low heat for 15 minutes. If the sauce dries out too much, add a little hot water.

Melt the remaining butter in a small skillet or frying pan, add the chicken giblets, and cook for 10 minutes, then season with salt and pepper.

Bring a large saucepan of salted water to a boil, add the pasta, and cook for 2–3 minutes, or until al dente. Drain, transfer to a warm soup tureen, then stir in the sauce and the chicken giblets. Stir, then sprinkle with grated Parmesan cheese to serve.

PAPPARDELLE AI FUNGHI
PAPPARDELLE WITH MUSHROOMS

AVERAGE

- Preparation time: *10 minutes*
- Cooking time: *20 minutes*
- Calories per serving: *480*
- *Serves 4*

INGREDIENTS

- 5–6 tablespoons extra virgin olive oil
- 1 clove garlic
- 1 lb 2 oz/500 g porcini (ceps) or cremini (chestnut) mushrooms, sliced
- 1 quantity fresh Pappardelle (see page 21)
- 1 small bunch fresh flat-leaf parsley, finely chopped
- salt and pepper
- grated Parmesan, to serve (optional)

Heat 4–5 tablespoons oil in a large skillet or frying pan, add the garlic, and let brown gently over low heat. Discard the garlic, add the mushrooms, season with salt, and cook for 2–3 minutes over high heat. Reduce the heat, cover, and cook for another 10 minutes.

Bring a large saucepan of salted water to a boil and add 1 tablespoon oil and the pappardelle. Cook 2–3 minutes, or until al dente. Add ¼ cup (2 fl oz/60 ml) of cooking water to the pan with the mushrooms. Drain the pasta and add it to the pan. Let cook for a few seconds, then add the parsley and pepper. Sprinkle with Parmesan, if using.

TAGLIATELLE
PROSCIUTTO E PISELLI
TAGLIATELLE WITH HAM AND PEAS

EASY

– Preparation time: *20 minutes*
– Cooking time: *20 minutes*
– Calories per serving: *735*
– *Serves 4*

INGREDIENTS

– 3 tablespoons (1½ oz/40 g) butter
– 1 small onion, finely chopped
– 1¾ cups (9 oz/250 g) peas
– 3½ oz/100 g Prosciutto Cotto, diced
– pinch of freshly grated nutmeg
– ⅔ cup (5 fl oz/150 ml) whipping cream
– ½ cup (1½ oz/40 g) grated Parmesan cheese
– 1 quantity fresh Tagliatelle (see page 21)
– salt and pepper

Melt 2 teaspoons (¼ oz/10 g) butter in a saucepan, add the onion and ¼ cup (2 fl oz/60 ml) of hot water, and cook gently without browning for 5–6 minutes, adding more water, if necessary. Add peas and a ladle of hot water and cook, covered, for about 4 minutes, or until tender.

Melt the remaining butter in a skillet or frying pan, add the ham, and cook for a few seconds, then add the peas and their cooking liquid. Season with salt, pepper, and nutmeg, pour in the cream, and cook for another 3–4 minutes. Remove from heat and add the cheese.

Bring a large saucepan of salted water to a boil, add the pasta, and cook for 2–3 minutes, or until al dente. Drain it, leaving it wet, then add it to the pan with the sauce. Toss together loosely, then serve with pepper. Serve immediately.

Tip: Reserve a ladle of the pasta cooking water. If the sauce is too thick when you stir the Parmesan cheese into the pasta, gradually add a small amount of cooking water until it is creamy in consistency.

GRATIN DI TAGLIATELLE

TAGLIATELLE GRATIN

EASY

- Preparation time: *10 minutes*
- Cooking time: *15 minutes*
- Calories per serving: *782*
- *Serves 4*

INGREDIENTS

- 1 quantity fresh
  Tagliatelle (see page 21)
- 3½ tablespoons (2 oz/50 g)
  butter, melted, plus extra for
  greasing
- 2 cups (9 oz/250 g) diced
  fontina cheese
- sprig of thyme, leaves only
- salt and pepper
- tomato sauce, to serve

Preheat the oven to 400°F/200°C/Gas Mark 6 and grease an ovenproof dish with butter. Bring a large saucepan of salted water to a boil, add the pasta, and cook for 2–3 minutes, or until al dente. Drain the pasta and dress it immediately with the melted butter and salt and pepper. Transfer to the prepared dish.

Sprinkle the cheese over the top, followed by a generous amount of pepper. Bake for about 10 minutes, or until the cheese is melting and bubbling and the pasta is starting to crisp. Sprinkle over the thyme leaves and serve with tomato sauce on the side.

Tip: To make the gratin creamier, cut the fontina into small pieces and leave it to soak in scant 1 cup (7 fl oz/200 ml) milk for at least 1 hour. Melt the mixture in a heavy saucepan, being careful not to boil it, and pour the creamy sauce over the tagliatelle. Bake in the oven.

SAGNE CHIETINE

ABRUZZAN PASTA WITH TOMATO SAUCE

AVERAGE

– Preparation time: *20 minutes*
– Cooking time: *45 minutes*
– Calories per serving: *469*
– *Serves 4*

INGREDIENTS

– generous ⅓ cup (3 fl oz/
  90 ml) olive oil
– 3 cloves garlic
– 9 (about 2¼ lb/1 kg) ripe
  tomatoes, skinned,
  seeded, and chopped
– 5–6 fresh basil leaves, plus
  extra or garnish
– ¼ red bell pepper, cut into
  very thin strips
– pinch of chili powder or
  dried oregano
– 1 quantity Fresh Egg Pasta
  (see page 17)
– salt
– finely grated pecorino
  cheese, to serve
– chili powder, to serve

Heat the oil in a large saucepan and gently cook the whole garlic cloves with the pepper strips over low heat. When the garlic and peppers are lightly browned, add the chopped tomatoes and simmer for about 30 minutes (the sauce should not be thick), then discard the garlic cloves. Add the basil leaves and some chili powder or oregano, stir, and remove from the heat.

Roll out the pasta dough into a thin sheet, cut into 1½-inch/4-cm-wide strips, then cut these into lozenges. Bring a large pan of salted water to a boil and add the pasta. Cover, then as soon as the water has returned to a full boil, drain the pasta and add it to the sauce in the pan. Serve with grated pecorino cheese and chili powder on the side.

FETTUCCINE VERDI

GREEN FETTUCCINE

ADVANCED

– Preparation time: *30 minutes*
  + 20 minutes drying and
  30 minutes resting
– Cooking time: *5 minutes*
– Calories per serving: *700*
– *Serves 2*

FOR THE PASTA

– 2 cups (2 oz/50 g) spinach,
  wilted and squeezed dry
– 2 cups (9 oz/250 g) "oo"
  flour
– 2 eggs
– 4 teaspoons olive or
  vegetable oil
– salt

FOR THE SAUCE

– 3½ tablespoons (2 oz/50 g)
  butter, melted
– a few fresh sage leaves
– ⅓ cup (1¼ oz/30 g) grated
  Parmesan cheese
– pepper

Squeeze out the spinach once more to get rid of any liquid and chop it very finely by hand with a sharp knife. Sift the flour into a large bowl or directly onto a clean work surface and make a well in the center.

Break the eggs into a bowl and beat them with a fork. Add the spinach and 1 teaspoon of oil and mix well. Pour the egg mixture into the center of the flour and gradually mix it, working from the center toward the edges. Work the mixture with your hands, loosening any leftover dough that remains on the pastry board with a spatula, and knead the dough for 5 minutes.

Wrap the dough in plastic wrap (clingfilm) and let rest for at least 30 minutes. Following the instructions on page 21, roll, dry, and cut the pasta into ¼-inch/5-mm strips, then arrange them in nests on a baking sheet.

Bring a large saucepan of salted water to a boil and add the remaining oil. Add the pasta and cook for 2–3 minutes, or until al dente. Reserve some of the pasta water, then drain well. Add the melted butter and sage plus most of the cheese. Add a splash of the water if the sauce seems dry. Season with pepper, then serve topped with the rest of the cheese.

Tip: The spinach can be replaced by the same amount of cooked borage or nettles, or replace the herbs with an envelope (sachet) of squid ink to make a pasta dough that can go with a fish sauce. Alternatively, flavor the dough with ¼ oz/10 g chopped chives or other aromatic herb.

FETTUCCINE CON SALSICCIA ALL'ACETO BALSAMICO
FETTUCCINE WITH SAUSAGE AND BALSAMIC VINEGAR

EASY

– Preparation time: *15 minutes*
– Cooking time: *30 minutes*
– Calories per serving: *405*
– *Serves 4*

INGREDIENTS

– 2 tablespoons (1¼ oz/30 g) butter
– 1 small onion, thinly sliced
– 3 oz/80 g Italian sausage, casings removed and finely crumbled
– 1 cup (7 oz/200 g) canned Italian chopped tomatoes, drained
– 2–3 sprigs fresh marjoram or oregano leaves, plus extra for garnishing
– 1 quantity fresh Fettuccine (see page 21)
– 1 tablespoon balsamic vinegar
– salt and pepper

Melt the butter in a large skillet or frying pan, add the onion, and cook gently until softened. Add the sausage meat and continue cooking for 10 minutes, stirring frequently. Add the tomatoes, followed by the marjoram, and season with salt and pepper. Cook for another 10 minutes.

Meanwhile, bring a large saucepan of salted water to a boil, add the pasta, and cook for 2–3 minutes, or until al dente. Reserve ½ cup (4 fl oz/120 ml) of the pasta water, then drain. Stir the pasta gently and briefly into the tomato and sausage sauce. Add a splash of the cooking water to loosen the pasta if it seems dry. Sprinkle with the vinegar and garnish with the marjoram. Serve immediately.

TAGLIERINI ALLA CREMA DI MASCARPONE E PEPERONI
MASCARPONE AND BELL PEPPER TAGLIERINI

EASY

– Preparation time: *10 minutes*
– Cooking time: *1 hour*
  15 minutes
– Calories per serving: *440*
– *Serves 2*

INGREDIENTS

– 1 yellow bell pepper
– 1 red bell peppers
– 2 tablespoons olive oil
– scant ½ cup (3½ oz/100 g)
  mascarpone cheese
– ½ quantity fresh Taglierini
  (see page 21)
– salt and pepper

Preheat the oven to 350°F/180°C/Gas Mark 4. Place the bell peppers in a roasting pan and roast them for about 1 hour. Take them out of the oven, wrap them in aluminum foil and let cool before removing the skin, stem (stalk), seeds, and pith. Slice them into thin strips.

Heat the oil in a large skillet or frying pan, add the roasted pepper strips, and heat them through briefly. Season with salt and pepper, add the mascarpone, and stir to blend into a creamy sauce.

Meanwhile, bring a large saucepan of salted water to a boil, add the pasta, and cook for 2–3 minutes, or until al dente. Drain and add the pasta to the sauce in the pan. Stir gently, transfer to a warm serving dish, and serve.

Tip: Make it even easier to remove the skin from the bell peppers and reduce the preparation time by brushing them with a little oil, placing them under a hot broiler (grill) and turning frequently. Put the peppers into a bowl, cover, and let cool before skinning them.

TAGLIATELLE AL RAGÙ DI SALSICCIA
TAGLIATELLE WITH SAUSAGE RAGU

AVERAGE

– Preparation time: *45 minutes*
– Cooking time: *40 minutes*
– Calories per serving: *960*
– *Serves 6*

INGREDIENTS

– 2 tablespoons olive oil
– 1 tablespoon (½ oz/15 g) butter
– 2 oz/50 g Italian cured bacon fat or pancetta, finely chopped
– 1 onion, finely chopped
– 1 stick celery, finely chopped
– 1 carrot, finely chopped
– 11 oz/300 g mixed lean beef and pork, finely chopped
– 3½ oz/100 g fresh Italian sausage, casings removed and crumbled
– 2 oz/50 g chicken livers, coarsely chopped
– 1 tablespoon milk
– 4 tablespoons dry white wine
– 1¼ cups (11 oz/300 g) tomato puree (passata)
– 1 quantity fresh Tagliatelle (see page 21)
– salt and pepper
– grated Parmesan cheese, to serve

Heat the oil in a deep skillet or frying pan. Add the butter and add the finely chopped bacon fat, onion, celery, and carrot. Cook gently for 5 minutes to brown lightly before adding the mixed lean meat, sausage, chicken livers, and milk. Stir, season with salt and pepper, and cook over high heat for 10 minutes, breaking the meat up well with a wooden spoon as it cooks. Add the wine and cook until it has evaporated. Add the tomato puree (passata) and 1 cup (8 fl oz/250 ml) water and simmer over low heat for 30 minutes until the sauce is thick and the meat is tender.

Bring a large saucepan of salted water to the boil. Add the pasta and boil for 2–3 minutes until al dente. Reserve ½ cup (4 fl oz/120 ml) of the water, then drain the pasta.

Stir the pasta into the ragu, add a splash of the cooking water if it seems dry, then serve with grated Parmesan on the side.

TAGLIATELLE WITH ASPARAGUS

– Preparation time: *10 minutes*
– Cooking time: *30 minutes*
– Calories per serving: *607*
– *Serves 4*

INGREDIENTS

– 1½ lb (8½ oz/700 g)
  asparagus
– 4 tablespoons (2 oz/60 g)
  butter
– 1 onion, finely chopped
– 1 quantity fresh Tagliatelle
  (see page 21)
– ½ cup (1½ oz/40 g) grated
  Parmesan cheese
– salt

Bring a saucepan of salted water to a boil. Trim the asparagus, cut off the tips, and boil them for 5–8 minutes, or until tender. Drain well.

Melt two-thirds of the butter in a saucepan, add the onion, and cook gently without letting it brown. Add the cooked asparagus tips and continue to cook gently, stirring occasionally, for 5 minutes.

Meanwhile, bring a large saucepan of salted water to a boil, add the pasta, and cook for 2–3 minutes, or until al dente. Drain the pasta and stir it into the asparagus mixture, adding the remaining butter and the grated Parmesan cheese. Serve immediately.

FETTUCCINE AL POLLO
E MANDORLE
FETTUCCINE WITH CHICKEN AND ALMONDS

AVERAGE

– Preparation time: *20 minutes*
– Cooking time: *25 minutes*
– Calories per serving: *960*
– *Serves 2*

INGREDIENTS

– 2 tablespoons (1¼ oz/30 g)
  butter
– 1 shallot, finely chopped
– 5 oz/150 g skinless boneless
  chicken breast, chopped into
  small pieces
– ¼ cup (1½ oz/40 g)
  unblanched almonds,
  coarsely chopped
– scant ½ cup (3½ fl oz/
  100 ml) dry white wine
– scant 1 cup (7 fl oz/200 ml)
  heavy (double) cream
– ½ quantity fresh Fettuccine
  (see page 21)
– ⅓ cup (1 oz/25 g) finely
  grated Parmesan cheese,
– salt and pepper

Melt the butter in a skillet or frying pan, then add
the shallot and cook gently for 5 minutes until softened.
Increase the heat, add the chicken and almonds,
then cook for 5 minutes, stirring often, until the meat
is browned all over. Pour in the wine, let it reduce
to a few tablespoons, then stir in the cream. Simmer over
low heat for 10 minutes, until the sauce has thickened,
then season with salt and pepper.

Bring a large saucepan of salted water to a boil, add
the pasta, and cook for 2–3 minutes, or until al dente.
Drain and transfer to a warm serving dish, then pour
the chicken sauce over it and toss together. Sprinkle
with the Parmesan. Serve immediately.

TAGLIATELLE AL SALMONE
TAGLIATELLE WITH SALMON

EASY

– Preparation time: *5 minutes*
– Cooking time: *10 minutes*
– Calories per serving: *607*
– *Serves 2*

INGREDIENTS

– 4 tablespoons (2 oz/60 g) butter
– 7 oz/200 g smoked salmon, chopped
– scant ½ cup (3½ fl oz/ 100 ml) heavy (double) cream
– 1 tablespoon whiskey
– juice of ½ lemon
– ½ quantity fresh Tagliatelle (see page 21)
– salt and pepper

Melt the butter in a medium saucepan. Stir in the salmon, cream, and whiskey. Cook over low heat for 2 minutes or until the salmon has turned opaque and the cream has thickened a little. Season with salt and pepper and 1 tablespoon lemon juice, or more, to taste.

Meanwhile, bring a large saucepan of salted water to a boil, add the pasta, and cook for 2–3 minutes, or until al dente. Drain, then add the pasta to the sauce and toss together gently. Transfer to a warm serving dish.

TAGLIATELLE,
FAVE E CALAMARETTI
TAGLIATELLE WITH FAVA BEANS AND SQUID

AVERAGE

– Preparation time: *25 minutes*
– Cooking time: *15 minutes*
– Calories per serving: *367*
– *Serves 4*

INGREDIENTS

– 3½ tablespoons (2 oz/50 g) butter
– 1 shallot, finely chopped
– scant ½ cup (3½ fl oz/ 100 ml) dry white wine
– 11 oz/300 g frozen fava (broad) beans, shelled (about ⅔ cup prepared)
– 14 oz/400 g squid, cleaned and cut into strips
– 1 quantity fresh Tagliatelle (see page 21)
– salt and pepper

Melt half the butter in a saucepan, add the shallot, and cook gently over low heat for 10 minutes until softened. Add the wine, let it reduce to a few tablespoons.

Add the beans and remaining butter, and cook over low heat, stirring occasionally, for 2 minutes. Add the squid rings, cover the pan, and cook for another minute, or until the squid has turned white and the beans are just tender. Be careful to avoid overcooking the squid. Season with salt and pepper.

Meanwhile, bring a large saucepan of salted water to a boil, add the pasta, and cook for 2–3 minutes, or until al dente. Drain the pasta and add to the squid and beans. Stir over the heat for 1 minute before serving.

Tip: Blanching the shelled beans for about 1 minute in boiling water and removing the skins will make them far more pleasant to eat and prettier on the plate. This can be done ahead of time, if you like.

STRACCI ALLE VONGOLE
STRACCI WITH CLAMS

– Preparation time: *30 minutes*
– Cooking time: *30 minutes*
– Calories per serving: *555*
– *Serves 4*

INGREDIENTS

– 1 quantity Fresh Egg Pasta
 (see page 17)
– 2¼ lb/1 kg clams
– 3 cloves garlic
– 4 tablespoons olive oil
– ¾ cup (7 oz/200 g) canned
 tomatoes, diced or chopped
– 2 tablespoons finely chopped
 fresh flat-leaf parsley
– salt and pepper

Roll out the pasta dough using a pasta machine until it is approximately ¹⁄₁₆ inch/1 mm thick. Cut into irregular shapes and set aside.

Rinse the clams thoroughly under running water and place in a skillet or frying pan with 2 garlic cloves and 2 tablespoons oil. Cook, covered, over high heat until the clams open. Take the clam meat out of the shells and strain the cooking liquid through a strainer (sieve) lined with cheesecloth (muslin). Set both aside.

Heat the remaining oil in a large saucepan, add the canned tomatoes and remaining garlic clove, and simmer gently. After 10 minutes, add a scant 1 cup (7 fl oz/200 ml) of the strained cooking liquid, season with salt and pepper, and cook over high heat for 5 minutes. Return the clams to the pan just before adding the pasta.

Bring a large saucepan of salted water to a boil, add the pasta, and cook for 2–3 minutes, or until al dente. Drain the pasta, add to the pan with the clam sauce, and heat through briefly. Sprinkle with chopped parsley and serve.

PAPPARDELLE
AL SUGO DI CONIGLIO
PAPPARDELLE WITH RABBIT AND TOMATO SAUCE

EASY

– Preparation time: *10 minutes*
– Cooking time: *35 minutes*
– Calories per serving: *520*
– *Serves 4*

INGREDIENTS

– 3 tablespoons oil
– 1 onion, finely chopped
– 1 stick celery, trimmed and finely chopped
– 2–3 sprigs fresh flat-leaf parsley, finely chopped
– 1 clove garlic, finely chopped
– 1 lb 2 oz/500 g rabbit, deboned and cut into small pieces
– 4 tablespoons dry white wine
– 1½ cups (¾ lb/350 g) tomato puree (passata)
– hot vegetable broth (stock) (optional)
– 1 quantity fresh Pappardelle (see page 21)
– salt and pepper

Heat the oil in a large saucepan over low heat and stir in the onion, celery, parsley, and garlic. Season with salt and pepper and cook gently for about 10 minutes. Add the rabbit meat and brown it for 5 minutes, then add the wine and cook over higher heat until it has evaporated. Stir in the tomato puree (passata) and cook for 20 minutes, adding hot broth to dilute the sauce, if necessary.

Bring a large saucepan of salted water to a boil, add the pasta, and cook for 2–3 minutes, or until al dente. Drain and stir into the hot sauce.

Tip: Rabbit is a very digestible meat with little fat, making it ideal for light, healthy sauces.

PAPPARDELLE AL GRANCHIO VELATE AL POMODORO

PAPPARDELLE WITH CREAMY CRAB AND TOMATO SAUCE

EASY

– Preparation time: *5 minutes*
– Cooking time: *30 minutes*
– Calories per serving: *1,035*
– *Serves 2*

INGREDIENTS

– 2 large ripe plum tomatoes
– olive oil, for cooking
– 1 small onion, finely
  chopped
– 1 cup (8 fl oz/250 ml) light
  (single) cream
– 1 tablespoon tomato puree
  (passata)
– 14 oz/400 g crabmeat
– ½ quantity fresh
  Pappardelle (see page 21)
– salt and pepper

Scald the tomatoes in boiling water for a few seconds, drain them, let cool, then skin them. Seed the tomatoes, chop them coarsely, and set aside.

Heat the oil in a large saucepan, add the onion, and cook gently until softened. Pour in the cream and tomato puree (passata) and season with salt and pepper. Place on the heat, bring to a boil, reduce the heat, and cook gently, stirring occasionally, until the cream is slightly thicker.

Remove the pan from the heat and strain the mixture through a fine-mesh strainer (sieve) into another pan. Add the crabmeat and tomatoes and heat gently; do not let it boil.

Bring a large saucepan of salted water to a boil, add the pasta, and cook for 2–3 minutes, or until al dente. Drain, transfer to a warm serving dish, and pour the sauce over it.

Tip: Drain any liquid from the crabmeat before using it and, if it is very wet, blot it dry with paper towels.

PAPPARDELLE ALLE CAPPESANTE
PAPPARDELLE WITH SCALLOPS

EASY

- Preparation time: *18 minutes*
- Cooking time: *25 minutes*
- Calories per serving: *555*
- *Serves 2*

INGREDIENTS

- 2 tablespoons olive oil
- 1 shallot, finely chopped
- 1 sprig fresh tarragon,
  finely chopped
- 12 scallops, shelled
- scant 1 cup (7 fl oz/200 ml)
  dry white wine
- ¾ cup (7 oz/200 g) canned
  chopped tomatoes
- ½ quantity fresh
  Pappardelle (see page 21)
- 1 tablespoon finely chopped
  fresh flat-leaf parsley
- salt and pepper

Heat the oil in a saucepan over medium heat. Add the shallot and tarragon and cook over low heat, stirring occasionally, for 5 minutes. Add the scallops, drizzle with the wine, and cook until the alcohol has evaporated. Simmer for 10 minutes, then add the tomatoes, season with salt and pepper, and simmer for another 5 minutes.

Bring a large saucepan of salted water to a boil, add the pasta, and cook for 2–3 minutes until al dente. Drain, tip the pasta into a warm serving dish, and pour the sauce over. Sprinkle with the parsley and serve immediately.

PAPPARDELLE CON CAVOLFIORE E GORGONZOLA

PAPPARDELLE WITH CAULIFLOWER AND GORGONZOLA

EASY

- Preparation time: *25 minutes*
- Cooking time: *25 minutes*
- Calories per serving: *555*
- *Serves 4*

INGREDIENTS

- 1½ cups (7 oz/200 g) cauliflower florets
- 1½ tablespoons (¾ oz/20 g) butter
- 5 oz/150 g Gorgonzola cheese, diced
- 3–4 tablespoons milk (optional)
- 2–3 tablespoons olive oil
- 1 clove garlic
- 1 tablespoon chopped thyme
- 1 quantity fresh Pappardelle (see page 21)
- ⅓ cup (1 oz/25 g) grated Parmesan cheese
- salt and pepper

Parboil the cauliflower in a saucepan of salted, boiling water for 5 minutes, then drain, reserving the cooking water.

Melt the butter with the Gorgonzola in a small saucepan over low heat, stirring constantly and adding a few tablespoons of milk, if necessary. Do not let the mixture boil. Remove the pan from the heat. Heat the oil in a shallow saucepan. Add the garlic clove and cook over low heat, stirring frequently, for a few minutes until lightly browned. Remove the garlic and discard.

Add the cauliflower to the pan and cook, stirring occasionally, for 5 minutes. Sprinkle with the thyme and season with salt and pepper.

Cook the pappardelle in the reserved cooking water, topped up with more boiling water, if necessary, for 2–3 minutes, until al dente. Drain, transfer to the pan with the cauliflower and stir. Stir in the Gorgonzola mixture, remove from the heat, and serve sprinkled with the grated Parmesan.

PAPPARDELLE ALLE NOCI
PAPPARDELLE WITH WALNUTS

EASY

– Preparation time: *10 minutes*
– Cooking time: *15 minutes*
– Calories per serving: *1,020*
– *Serves 2*

INGREDIENTS

– 3 tablespoons (1½ oz/40 g) butter
– ⅔ cup (3 oz/80 g) walnuts, coarsely chopped
– 1 tablespoon pink peppercorns, freshly ground
– 1 tablespoon chopped fresh flat-leaf parsley
– ½ quantity fresh Pappardelle (see page 21)
– salt

Melt the butter in a large saucepan, then add the walnuts and peppercorns. Cook for 4 minutes over low heat, stirring continuously. Remove from the heat and add the chopped parsley.

Bring a large saucepan of salted water to a boil, add the pasta, and cook for 2–3 minutes, or until al dente. Drain and add the pasta to the walnut sauce, stirring until it's well combined. Transfer to a hot serving dish and serve immediately.

Tip: If you have the time and patience, scald the walnuts in boiling water for a few seconds to get rid of the bitter taste given by the brown membrane. Let the walnuts cool, then skin them.

TAGLIATELLE BICOLORI AL SUGO DI FAGIOLI
TWO-TONE TAGLIATELLE WITH BEAN SAUCE

AVERAGE

– Preparation time: *20 minutes*
– Cooking time: *1 hour
20 minutes*
– Calories per serving: *819*
– *Serves 4*

INGREDIENTS

– 1½ lb (½-¾ oz/15-20 g)
cranberry (borlotti) beans,
shelled (about 3½ cups
prepared)
– 1–1½ tablespoons butter
– 2 tablespoons olive oil
– 3 oz/80 g pancetta,
finely chopped
– 1 onion, finely chopped
– fresh flat-leaf parsley,
finely chopped
– 1 clove garlic, finely chopped
– 1 tablespoon tomato paste
(UK tomato puree)
– ¾ cup (6 fl oz/175 ml) hot
vegetable broth (stock)
– ½ quantity fresh Tagliatelle
(see page 21)
– ½ quantity Green Tagliatelle
(see page 32)
– grated Parmesan cheese,
to serve
– salt and pepper

Bring a large saucepan of salted water to a boil, add
the beans, and cook for about 1 hour, or until they
are just tender.

Melt 1 tablespoon butter in a large saucepan with
the oil, add the pancetta, onion, parsley, and garlic,
and cook for a few minutes, stirring continuously,
until lightly browned.

Stir the tomato paste (UK tomato puree) into the hot
broth (stock), add to the saucepan, and simmer for
a few minutes. Add the beans (one-third of these
can be pureed, if desired) and continue cooking until
the sauce is fairly thick. Remove from the heat and season
with salt and pepper.

Meanwhile, bring a large saucepan of salted water
to a boil, add the pastas, and cook for 2–3 minutes,
or until al dente. Drain the pastas and mix them with
the bean sauce. Serve with grated Parmesan cheese
on the side.

PAPPARDELLE ALL'ARETINA
AREZZO-STYLE PAPPARDELLE

ADVANCED

– Preparation time: *45 minutes*
– Cooking time: *1 hour*
  50 minutes
– Calories per serving: *1,040*
– *Serves 2*

INGREDIENTS

– 2 tablespoons oil
– 1 (2¼ lb/1 kg) duckling,
  washed and cut into 8
  pieces, with the liver reserved
– 3½ oz/100 g pancetta, cubed
– 1 onion, finely chopped
– 1 stick celery, finely chopped
– 1 carrot, finely chopped
– scant ½ cup (3½ fl oz/
  100 ml) dry white wine
– 1½ cups (14 oz/400 g)
  canned tomatoes
– ¾ quantity fresh
  Pappardelle (see page 21)
– salt and pepper
– butter, to serve
– grated Parmesan cheese,
  to serve

Heat 1 tablespoon oil in a large skillet or frying pan.
Add the duck pieces and brown for 5 minutes on each
side, until golden. Spoon away the excess duck fat
as the duck cooks. Set the duck aside.

Add the remaining oil, the pancetta, onion, celery,
and carrot. Cook over low heat for 10 minutes until
the vegetables are softened. Return the duck to the pan,
then pour in the wine. Simmer for a few minutes until
the wine is reduced.

Add the tomatoes, season with salt and pepper, and cook
for about 1 hour 20 minutes, covered. Add the reserved
liver and cook for another 10 minutes, or until the meat
is falling from the bones and the sauce is rich and thick.

Bring a large saucepan of salted water to a boil, add
the pasta, and cook for 2–3 minutes, or until al dente.
Drain and transfer to a warm serving dish, stir in a little
butter, then add the sauce. Sprinkle with grated cheese
and serve.

*Tip: This kind of pasta is generally made with a sauce
based on duck, hare, or wild boar. The meat is usually served
as a main course, whereas the sauce is used for the first course
of pasta.*

TAGLIERINI ALLA GRANCEOLA

TAGLIERINI WITH CRAB

AVERAGE

– Preparation time: *45 minutes*
  + 30 minutes resting
– Cooking time: *1 hour*
– Calories per serving: *1,174*
– *Serves 2*

INGREDIENTS

– 1 (1½–1¾ lb/700–800 g)
  fresh crab, legs and emptied
  claw shells reserved
– 4 tablespoons oil
– butter, for cooking
– 1 clove garlic
– 1 tablespoon brandy
– ½ quantity fresh
  Taglierini (see page 21)
– salt and freshly ground
  white pepper

Twist off the crab's legs and claws. Open the crab's body by levering the underside away from the reddish top and extract the meat, using a crab pick where necessary. Discard the feathery gills. Reserve the crab roe if present.

To make a crab broth (stock), put the crab legs and claw shells in a saucepan, add 2 cups (16 fl oz/475 ml) cold water, and boil for about 20 minutes. Remove from the heat. Strain and season with just a little salt. Heat the oil and a knob of butter in a pan, brown the garlic clove, then discard it. Add the crabmeat to the pan, stir well, and sprinkle with the brandy. Cook until it has evaporated. Pour in a scant ½ cup (3½ fl oz/100 ml) of the crab broth, simmer to reduce a little, and taste to check the seasoning, adding more salt, if needed.

Bring a large pan of salted water to a boil, add the pasta, and cook for 2–3 minutes, or until al dente. Drain well, transfer the pasta to a warm serving dish, and add the crab sauce. Sprinkle with freshly ground white pepper. Serve hot.

AVERAGE

- Preparation time: *30 minutes*
- Cooking time: *20 minutes*
- Calories per serving: *628*
- *Serves 4*

FOR THE PASTA

- 3¼ cups (14 oz/400 g) all-purpose (plain) flour
- 2 eggs
- 1–2 tablespoons grated Parmesan cheese

FOR THE SAUCE

- 6 tablespoons (3 oz/80 g) butter
- pinch of freshly grated nutmeg
- scant 1 cup (2½–3 oz/ 70–80 g) grated Parmesan cheese
- vegetable or chicken broth (stock), to taste
- 1 white Alba truffle
- salt and pepper

First, make the pasta dough. Sift the flour into a mound in a large bowl or on a clean work surface, make a well in the center, and break the eggs into it. Sprinkle with Parmesan cheese and add enough water—about ⅓ cup (3 fl oz/90 ml)—to obtain a fairly firm mixture. Gradually incorporate the eggs and liquid and knead the dough thoroughly. Roll it out into a thin sheet and, using a sharp knife, slice the roll into taglierini about ⅛ inch/3 mm wide.

To make the sauce, melt the butter in a small saucepan, add the grated nutmeg and the cheese, and dilute it with a little broth (stock) and cook over low heat for a few minutes until the sauce is a good consistency. Check the seasoning and add salt and pepper, if necessary. Remove from the heat.

Bring a large pan of salted water to a boil, add the pasta, and cook for 2–3 minutes, or until al dente. Drain the pasta and transfer it to a warmed serving dish, then stir in the sauce. Sprinkle with the truffle shavings and serve.

"NANA" SULLE PAPPARDELLE
PAPPARDELLE WITH DUCK RAGU

ADVANCED

– Preparation time: *30 minutes*
– Cooking time: *50 minutes*
– Calories per serving: *1,026*
– *Serves 2*

INGREDIENTS

– 3 tablespoons oil
– 1 (2¼ lb/1 kg) duckling,
  meat chopped, liver and
  gizzard reserved and
  chopped
– butter, for cooking
– 1 carrot, finely chopped
– 1 onion, finely chopped
– 1 stick celery, finely chopped
– 1 tablespoon fresh flat-leaf
  parsley, finely chopped
– 1 teaspoon thyme leaves,
  chopped
– 1 teaspoon marjoram leaves,
  chopped
– 5 oz/150 g ground
  (minced) veal (optional)
– scant ½ cup (3½ fl oz/
  100 ml) dry white wine
– 1 tablespoon tomato paste
  (tomato puree)
– 2–3 ripe tomatoes, skinned
  and diced (optional)
– ½ quantity fresh
  Pappardelle (see page 21)
– salt and pepper
– grated Parmesan cheese,
  to serve

Heat 2 tablespoons oil in a skillet or frying pan and brown the chopped duck over high heat. Season with salt and pepper and continue cooking over low heat until the meat is well browned. Remove the pan from the heat, remove the duck pieces, and set aside.

Melt a little butter in the same pan, add the carrot, onion, celery, parsley, thyme, and marjoram, and cook gently. After a few minutes, add the duck liver and gizzard and the ground veal, if using, and cook until browned. Season with salt and pepper.

Cook for 10 minutes, then add the duck pieces and the wine and gradually add the tomato paste (tomato puree) diluted in a little hot water or broth (stock). Cook for about 30 minutes. Add the fresh tomatoes, if using.

Bring a large saucepan of salted water to a boil, add the pasta, and cook for 2–3 minutes, or until al dente. Drain, transfer to a warm serving dish, and pour the sauce over it. Sprinkle with Parmesan cheese. The duck meat can then be served as a main course, or it can be placed on top of the pasta and served as a one-dish meal.

LASAGNE

LASAGNE AL PESTO
LASAGNE WITH PESTO

AVERAGE

– Preparation time: *15 minutes*
– Cooking time: *30–40 minutes*
– Calories per portion: *460*
– *Serves 4*

INGREDIENTS

– 1 quantity Fresh Egg Pasta
  (see page 17)
– 1 tablespoon olive or
  vegetable oil, plus extra for
  greasing
– 1½ quantities Béchamel
  Sauce (see page 87)
– scant 1 cup (5 oz/150 g)
  good-quality fresh pesto, plus
  extra to serve
– ½ cup (1½ oz/40 g) finely
  grated Parmesan cheese
– 2 tablespoons pine nuts
– salt

STEP 1

Preheat the oven to 350°F/180°C/Gas Mark 4 and lightly
grease an 8 x 9½-inch/20 x 24-cm ovenproof dish. Roll
out the egg pasta dough on a clean work surface into
a sheet; it should not be too thin. Using a pasta-cutting
wheel with a smooth edge, cut the sheet into rectangles
measuring about 4 x 7 inches/10 x 18 cm.

STEP 2

Bring a large saucepan of salted water to a boil with
1 tablespoon oil, then add the pasta, a few noodles
(sheets) at a time. When the noodles rise to the top
of the pan, remove them with a slotted spoon and spread
them on a clean dish towel or parchment (baking) paper.

STEP 3

Cover the bottom of the dish with 2 lasagne noodles,
then cover with a thin layer of béchamel followed
by a few teaspoons of the pesto and a sprinkling
of Parmesan. Repeat the layers, creating 6 layers
of pasta in all, and finishing with a layer of béchamel.
Sprinkle the pine nuts on top.

STEP 4

Bake the lasagne for 30–40 minutes, until golden
and hot through. Let stand for 3–4 minutes to make
serving easier.

LASAGNE ALLA BOLOGNESE
LASAGNE WITH MEAT SAUCE

AVERAGE

– Preparation time: *30 minutes*
– Cooking time: *1 hour
20 minutes*
– Calories per serving: *510*
– *Serves 6*

INGREDIENTS

– 3 tablespoons oil, plus extra
for boiling
– 1 carrot, finely chopped
– 1 onion, finely chopped
– 11 oz/300 g beef, very finely
chopped or ground (minced)
– 4 tablespoons dry white wine
– 2 ripe tomatoes, skinned,
seeded, and chopped
– 1 quantity fresh Lasagne
(see page 73)
– butter, for greasing and
dotting
– 2 cups (16 fl oz/475 ml)
Béchamel Sauce (see
page 87)
– scant 1 cup (2½ oz/70 g)
grated Parmesan cheese
– salt and pepper

Heat the oil in a saucepan, add the carrot and onion, and cook gently until softened. Add the beef and cook until browned, in batches if necessary. Return all the beef to the pan, pour in the wine, and cook until it has evaporated. Season with salt to taste, add the tomatoes, and simmer for 30 minutes. Season with pepper.

Preheat the oven to 350°F/180°C/Gas Mark 4 and grease an ovenproof dish with butter.

Bring a large saucepan of salted water to a boil with the oil, then add the pasta, a few noodles (sheets) at a time. When the noodles rise to the top of the pan, remove them with a slotted spoon and spread them out on a clean dish towel or parchment (baking) paper.

Line the bottom of the prepared dish with lasagne noodles, spoon some of the meat sauce over them, followed by some béchamel sauce, then sprinkle with some of the grated Parmesan cheese and dot with butter. Follow with a layer of lasagne and continue layering until all the ingredients have been used, ending with meat sauce and, finally, béchamel sauce. Bake for 30 minutes. Let stand for a few minutes, then serve hot.

Tip: A little milk is traditionally added to the meat sauce as it cooks, making the taste milder and resulting in a softer, more velvety texture.

LASAGNE VEGETARIANE

VEGETARIAN LASAGNE

AVERAGE

– Preparation time: *40 minutes*
– Cooking time: *40 minutes*
– Calories per serving: *440*
– *Serves 4*

INGREDIENTS

– butter, for greasing
– 1 quantity fresh Lasagne
  (see page 73)
– 5 tablespoons olive oil, for
  frying
– 2 scallions (spring onions),
  chopped
– 7 oz/200 g pumpkin, cut into
  ½-inch/1-cm pieces (about
  1¾ cup prepared)
– 2 zucchini (courgettes),
  chopped
– 1¾ cups (7 oz/200 g) cherry
  tomatoes, halved
– 1 small sprig fresh rosemary,
  chopped, plus extra for
  garnish
– 4 tablespoons double (heavy)
  cream
– 7 oz/200 g stracchino or
  taleggio cheese
– 2 small sprigs fresh
  marjoram, chopped
– 1¼ cups (3½ oz/100 g)
  grated Parmesan cheese
– salt and pepper

Preheat the oven to 350°F/180°C/Gas Mark 4 and lightly grease an 8 x 9½-inch/20 x 24-cm ovenproof dish with butter.

Heat 4 tablespoons oil in a large saucepan, add the scallions (spring onions), and cook them gently for 2–3 minutes. Add the pumpkin and cook, covered, for 5–6 minutes. Add the zucchini (courgettes), cherry tomatoes, and chopped rosemary and season with salt. Cook over medium heat for another 10 minutes, or until the vegetables are just tender and turning golden.

Meanwhile, mix together the cream, stracchino cheese, marjoram and a pinch of salt.

Bring a large saucepan of salted water to a boil with 1 tablespoon oil, then add the pasta, a few noodles at a time. When the noodles rise to the top of the pan, remove them with a slotted spoon and spread on a clean dish towel or parchment (baking) paper.

Arrange one-third of the vegetables on the bottom of the prepared dish, followed by a layer of pasta, some of the cheese sauce, vegetables, and the Parmesan cheese. Continue layering you have three layers of pasta, then finish with the remaining vegetables and cheese. Sprinkle over the rosemary leaves and season with pepper. Bake the lasagne for about 30 minutes, or until golden and hot through, then serve.

LASAGNE DORATE

HAM AND EGG LASAGNE

EASY

– Preparation time: *45 minutes*
– Cooking time: *45 minutes*
– Calories per serving: *610*
– *Serves 6*

INGREDIENTS

– 1 tablespoon oil
– 1 quantity fresh Lasagne
  (see page 73)
– 2 cups (16 fl oz/475 ml)
  Béchamel Sauce (see
  page 87)
– 2 egg yolks, lightly beaten
– grated Parmesan cheese,
  to taste
– 4 oz/120 g ham, finely
  chopped
– 4 hard-boiled eggs, sliced
– 3½ tablespoons (2 oz/50 g)
  butter, plus extra for
  greasing
– 9 oz/250 g fontina cheese,
  thinly sliced
– salt

Preheat the oven to 350°F/180°C/Gas Mark 4 and grease an ovenproof dish with butter.

Bring a large saucepan of salted water to a boil with 1 tablespoon oil, then add the pasta a few noodles (sheets) at a time. When the noodles rise to the top of the pan, remove them with a slotted spoon and spread on a clean dish towel or parchment (baking) paper.

Heat the béchamel sauce in a small saucepan, remove from the heat, and beat in the egg yolks, followed by a little grated Parmesan cheese and the chopped ham.

Line the bottom of the ovenproof dish with a layer of lasagne noodles (sheets). Cover the lasagne with a layer of hard-boiled egg slices, dot with butter, and add some strips of fontina cheese over these, followed by some grated Parmesan cheese, and a layer of béchamel sauce. Continue layering the ingredients until you have used them all, ending with a layer of sauce dotted with butter. Bake for 30 minutes, then serve hot.

Tip: To peel eggs easily, cool them under running cold water as soon as they are cooked, then roll them on a work surface to crack the shells and let soak in cold water for about 10 minutes. The water will seep between the shell and the egg white, making it easier to peel off the shell.

LASAGNE CON CREMA
DI PARMIGIANO E FUNGHI
CREAMY MUSHROOM AND PARMESAN LASAGNE

Bring a large saucepan of salted water to a boil with 1 tablespoon oil, then add the pasta, a few noodles (sheets) at a time. When the noodles rise to the top of the pan, remove them with a slotted spoon and spread on a clean dish towel or parchment (baking) paper.

Gently melt 5 tablespoons (2½ oz/70 g) butter with the sage leaves, discarding them when they start to brown. Pour in the cream and bring to a gentle boil. Remove from the heat, add the grated Parmesan cheese, stir, and set aside.

Heat 2 tablespoons oil in a saucepan and brown the garlic clove lightly, then discard it. Add the mushrooms and a pinch of salt and cook for 30 minutes. Preheat the oven to 350°F/180°C/Gas Mark 4 and grease an ovenproof dish with butter.

Layer the ingredients in the dish, starting with lasagne noodles, followed by cheese sauce, and then the mushrooms. Continue layering until all the ingredients have been used, ending with a layer of the pasta. Distribute the remaining butter in small pieces on the surface and bake for 20 minutes. Let stand for a few minutes, then serve hot.

Tip: To prevent the lasagne on top of the dish from becoming dry when baked, cover the dish with a sheet of aluminum foil for the first 10 minutes.

LASAGNE ALLE MELANZANE E RICOTTA

EGGPLANT AND RICOTTA LASAGNE

AVERAGE

– Preparation time: *15 minutes + 30 minutes resting*
– Cooking time: *1 hour*
– Calories per serving: *513*
– *Serves 4*

INGREDIENTS

– butter, for greasing
– 1 large eggplant (aubergine)
– 1 tablespoon oil, plus extra for brushing and drizzling
– 1 quantity fresh Lasagne (see page 73)
– scant ½ cup (2 oz/50 g) pine nuts, finely chopped
– ⅔ cup (5 oz/150 g) ricotta cheese
– ½ cup (4 fl oz/120 ml) tomato puree (passata)
– fresh basil leaves
– salt
– grated Parmesan cheese, to serve

Preheat the broiler (grill) or the oven to 350°F/180°C/ Gas Mark 4 and grease an ovenproof dish with butter. Cut the eggplant (aubergine) into slices, place these in a colander, sprinkle with salt, and let drain for 30 minutes, then rinse them under running cold water and pat dry with paper towels. Brush the slices with oil and broil until tender.

Bring a large saucepan of salted water to a boil with 1 tablespoon oil, then add the pasta, a few noodles (sheets) at a time. When the noodles rise to the top of the pan, remove them with a slotted spoon and spread on a clean dish towel or parchment (baking) paper.

Cover the bottom of the dish with half the lasagne noodles, followed by half the eggplant slices, then sprinkle with some of the pine nuts, and crumble half the ricotta cheese on top, followed by 4 tablespoons tomato puree (passata), and some basil leaves. Drizzle over a little oil. Place the remaining pasta on top in another layer and cover with the remaining ingredients. Top with grated Parmesan cheese and bake in the oven for about 40 minutes. Serve hot.

Tip: For a more creamy texture, mix the ricotta cheese with a scant ½ cup (3½ fl oz/100 ml) whole (full-fat) milk or light (single) cream. You can also flavor the tomato puree by adding a finely chopped shallot, a pinch of sugar, 3 tablespoons oil, and a pinch of salt and cooking for 5–6 minutes.

LASAGNE TRICOLORI

TRICOLOR LASAGNE

AVERAGE

– Preparation time: *40 minutes*
– Cooking time: *1 hour
20 minutes*
– Calories per serving: *463*
– *Serves 6*

INGREDIENTS

– 1 quantity fresh Lasagne
  (see page 73)
– 2 cups (1 lb/450 g)
  ricotta cheese
– 2 lb/900 g spinach
– 2 tablespoons olive oil
– 1 clove garlic
– ¾ cup (6 fl oz/175 ml)
  tomato puree (passata)
– 3 tablespoons (1½ oz/40 g)
  butter, plus extra for
  greasing
– 1 cup (3 oz/80 g) grated
  pecorino cheese
– salt and pepper

Preheat the oven to 350°F/180°C/Gas Mark 4 and lightly grease an 8 x 9½-inch/20 x 24-cm ovenproof dish with butter. Push the ricotta cheese through a strainer (sieve) and season it with salt and pepper. Divide it into 3 equal portions.

Heat a large saucepan over medium-high heat and add the spinach. Cover and let the spinach cook for 1½ minutes, stirring once or twice during cooking, until wilted. Drain in a colander, then cool under cold water. Drain again, then squeeze out the liquid.

Chop the spinach and cook it in a skillet or frying pan with 1 tablespoon olive oil, the garlic clove, and a pinch of salt for 3–4 minutes, until any remaining moisture has evaporated. Mix the spinach with one of the ricotta portions, then mix the tomato puree (passata) with another, and keep the last one white.

Bring a large saucepan of salted water to a boil with oil, then add the pasta, a few noodles (sheets) at a time. When the noodles rise to the top of the pan, remove them with a slotted spoon and spread out on a clean dish towel or parchment (baking) paper.

Line the bottom of the dish with lasagna noodles and cover with the spinach ricotta cheese, then sprinkle with a quarter of the pecorino cheese. Cover with a layer of pasta and top this with the plain white ricotta cheese, followed by more pecorino cheese. Finish with a layer of pasta, then spread the tomato ricotta mix on top, plus more pecorino. Dot butter over the surface and bake for 40 minutes, or until crisp at the edges, golden and heated through. Serve.

LASAGNE AI CARCIOFI E FUNGHI

ARTICHOKE AND MUSHROOM LASAGNE

AVERAGE

– Preparation time: *40 minutes*
– Cooking time: *1 hour*
– Calories per serving: *443*
– *Serves 6*

INGREDIENTS

– 1¼ oz/30 g dried porcini
  (ceps)
– 10 baby artichokes
– juice of 1 lemon
– 3 tablespoons oil
– ½ onion, finely chopped
– 1 clove garlic, finely chopped
– 1 quantity fresh Lasagne
  (see page 73)
– ½ cup (1½ oz/40 g) grated
  Parmesan cheese
– salt and pepper

FOR THE BÉCHAMEL

– 2 tablespoons (1 oz/30 g)
  butter, plus extra for
  greasing
– 2 tablespoons all-purpose
  (plain) flour
– 2 cups (16 fl oz/475 ml)
  milk
– grated Parmesan cheese,
  to taste
– salt and pepper

Soak the dried porcini (ceps) in a bowl of lukewarm water. Slice the raw artichokes lengthwise and place in a bowl of water mixed with lemon juice. Heat 2 tablespoons oil in a large saucepan, add the onion and garlic, and cook gently until softened. Add the drained artichokes and brown them lightly before moistening them with a sprinkling of lukewarm water. Season with salt and pepper. When they are cooked halfway, squeeze the porcini dry and add them to the pan.

Make the béchamel sauce. Melt the butter in a small saucepan, add the flour and stir well, cooking until the flour has browned lightly. Gradually add the milk, stirring continuously. Continue cooking and stirring the sauce for 10 minutes, then remove from the heat, season with a little salt and pepper, and stir in the grated Parmesan cheese.

Preheat the oven to 350°F/180°C/Gas Mark 4 and grease an ovenproof dish with butter. Bring a large saucepan of salted water to a boil with 1 tablespoon oil, then add the pasta, a few noodles (sheets) at a time. When the noodles rise to the top of the pan, remove them with a slotted spoon and spread them out on a clean dish towel or parchment (baking) paper.

Layer the ingredients in the prepared dish in the following order: béchamel sauce, pasta, artichokes, mushrooms, continuing to layer until all the ingredients have been use, ending with a layer of sauce sprinkled with grated Parmesan cheese. Bake for 30 minutes. Remove from the oven and let rest before serving.

LASAGNE AL SAPORE DI MARE

SEAFOOD LASAGNE

AVERAGE

– Preparation time: *40 minutes*
– Cooking time: *30 minutes*
– Calories per serving: *360*
– *Serves 6*

INGREDIENTS

– butter, for greasing
– 2 tablespoons olive oil
– 1 quantity fresh Lasagne
  (see page 73)
– 7 oz/200 g scallops
– 4 tablespoons dry white wine
– 1 cup (8 fl oz/250 ml) light
  (single) cream
– ½ bunch fresh chives,
  chopped
– ½ cup (1½ oz/40 g) grated
  semi-mature pecorino
  cheese
– 7 oz/200 g crabmeat
– ¾ cup (6 fl oz/180 ml) pesto
  (see page 172)
– 2 canned Italian tomatoes,
  diced
– salt and pepper

Preheat the oven to 350°F/180°C/Gas Mark 4 and grease an ovenproof dish with butter.

Bring a large saucepan of salted water to a boil with 1 tablespoon oil, then add the pasta, a few noodles (sheets) at a time. When the noodles rise to the top of the pan, remove them with a slotted spoon and spread them out on a clean dish towel or parchment (baking) paper.

Heat the remaining oil in a saucepan over low heat, add the scallops, and cook for 1 minute, then turn them over and cook for another 1 minute. Remove the scallops from the pan and keep warm.

Pour the wine into the saucepan used for cooking the scallops and cook until it has reduced by half, add the cream and chives, and reduce the liquid by half again. Remove from the heat, stir in the grated pecorino cheese and the crabmeat. Season with salt and pepper. Mix the pesto with the diced tomatoes.

In the prepared dish, start with a layer of pasta, follow it with a layer of crab sauce and then some of the scallops. Continue layering, ending with a layer of pasta. Pour the pesto all over the surface. Put the dish into the preheated oven, turn the oven off, and let stand for 10 minutes. Serve warm.

LASAGNE AI FUNGHI PORCINI
LASAGNE WITH PORCINI

- Preparation time: *25 minutes*
- Cooking time: *50 minutes*
- Calories per serving: *360*
- *Serves 6*

INGREDIENTS

- 3 tablespoons oil
- 2 cloves garlic, crushed
- 1 lb 2 oz/500 g fresh ceps porcini (ceps), sliced
- 1 teaspoon thyme leaves
- scant ½ cup (3½ fl oz/ 100 ml) dry white wine
- 1 quantity Béchamel Sauce (see page 87)
- pinch of freshly grated nutmeg
- 1 quantity fresh Lasagne (see page 73)
- ⅔ cup (2 oz/50 g) grated Parmesan cheese
- 2 tablespoons (1 oz/30 g) butter, plus extra for greasing
- salt and pepper

Preheat the oven to 350°F/180°C/Gas Mark 4 and grease an ovenproof dish with butter. Heat 2 tablespoons oil in a saucepan, add the garlic, and cook until browned, then discard. Add the mushrooms, sprinkle with thyme, and pour in the wine. Cook until it has evaporated. Season with salt and pepper and cook gently for 10 minutes until the mushrooms are tender; cover the pan if they dry out too much.

Season the béchamel sauce with a pinch of nutmeg.

Bring a large saucepan of salted water to a boil with the oil, then add the pasta, a few noodles (sheets) at a time. When the noodles rise to the top of the pan, remove them with a slotted spoon and spread them out on a clean dish towel or parchment (baking) paper.

Cover the bottom of the prepared dish with a layer of pasta, followed by mushrooms, béchamel sauce, and grated Parmesan cheese. Continue layering, using all the ingredients, finishing with béchamel sauce on the top. Dot the butter on the surface. Bake for about 20 minutes, then serve hot.

LASAGNE DI CARNEVALE
CARNIVAL LASAGNE

AVERAGE

- Preparation time: *30 minutes*
- Cooking time: *40 minutes*
- Calories per serving: *670–502*
- *Serves 6-8*

INGREDIENTS

- 5 tablespoons olive oil, plus extra for frying
- 1 stick celery, diced
- 1 carrot, diced
- 1 onion, diced
- 9 oz/250 g Italian sausages, cut into bite-size pieces
- 3¼ cups (25 fl oz/750 ml) tomato puree (passata)
- 5½ oz/150 g ground (minced) pork
- 3½ oz/100 g ground (minced) veal
- ⅓ cup (1 oz/30 g) stale bread crumbs, moistened in water and squeezed dry
- 4 eggs
- ⅔ cup (2 oz/50 g) grated Pecorino cheese
- ½ quantity fresh Lasagne (see page 73)
- ¾ cup (9 oz/200 g) ricotta cheese
- 2 oz/50 g Neapolitan salami or pepperoni, sliced
- 5½ oz/150 g caciocavallo, scamorza, or provolone cheese, sliced
- semolina, for sprinkling
- salt

Heat 4 tablespoons oil in a saucepan, add the celery, carrot, and onion and cook gently for 5 minutes. Add the sausage and cook for a few minutes until they brown. Pour over the tomato puree (passata), season with salt, cover, and cook over low heat for 30 minutes.

Meanwhile, put the pork, veal, bread crumbs, 1 egg, and 1 tablespoon grated pecorino cheese into a bowl with a pinch of salt. Work the ingredients together and shape the mixture into about 40 hazelnut-size patties. Heat 2 tablespoons of oil in a skillet or frying pan until hot, add the patties and cook for 3–4 minutes, turning them over so that all sides are browned. Set aside, then add to the tomato sausage sauce once it's ready.

Preheat the oven to 350°F/180°C/Gas Mark 4. Boil the remaining 3 eggs for 10 minutes. Cool under cold water, then peel and slice.

Bring a large saucepan of salted water to a boil with 1 tablespoon oil, then add the pasta a few noodles (sheets) at a time. When the noodles rise to the top of the pan, remove them with a slotted spoon and spread them out on a clean dish towel or parchment (baking) paper.

Spread a thin layer of sauce into an ovenproof dish, followed by a layer of pasta, then another layer of sauce with half the ricotta cheese, some salami, sliced egg, caciocavallo cheese, and the remaining pecorino cheese. Continue layering until you've made 3 layers of pasta in total and finishing with the meat sauce, salami, eggs and cheese. Bake, loosely covered with aluminum foil, for 20 minutes, then uncovered for another 20 minutes. Serve hot.

LASAGNE DI GRANO SARACENO CON BROCCOLI

BUCKWHEAT LASAGNE WITH BROCCOLI

ADVANCED

– Preparation time: *30 minutes*
  + 30 minutes resting
– Cooking time: *1 hour*
– Calories per serving: *540*
– *Serves 8*

FOR THE PASTA

– ⅔ cup (3½ oz/100 g)
  buckwheat flour
– 1⅔ cups (7 oz/200 g)
  "00" flour
– 3 eggs
– salt

FOR THE FILLING

– 2¼ lb/1 kg broccoli florets
– 1 savoy cabbage
– 2 tablespoons (1 oz/25 g)
  butter, plus extra for
  greasing
– 2 oz/50 g cubed pancetta
– 2 shallots, thinly sliced
– ½ cup (4 oz /120 g)
  ricotta cheese
– ⅔ cup (2 oz/50 g) grated
  Parmesan cheese
– freshly grated nutmeg
– 1 quantity Béchamel Sauce
  (see page 87)
– 3½ oz/100 g Emmental
  cheese, diced
– ½ teaspoon salt
– pepper

Sift both types of flour together into a mound on a clean work surface, make a well in the center, and break the eggs into it. Gradually combine the eggs with the flour and knead to make a smooth, elastic dough. Wrap in plastic wrap (clingfilm) and let rest for 30 minutes.

Bring a large saucepan of salted water to a boil. Add the broccoli florets and cook for 2 minutes, or until bright green but still crisp. Lift from the pan with a slotted spoon, cool under cold water, then drain well. Repeat with the cabbage.

Melt the butter in a large saucepan and add the pancetta and shallots. Cook gently for a few minutes before adding the cabbage and broccoli, then cover the pan and cook for 5 minutes, stirring now and again, until softened. Let cool before stirring in the ricotta, grated Parmesan cheese, nutmeg, salt and pepper.

Roll out the pasta, cut into noodles (sheets), and leave to dry for 20 minutes. Bring a large saucepan of salted water to a boil and add a teaspoon of oil, then add the pasta a few noodles (sheets) at a time. When the noodles rise to the top of the pan, remove them with a slotted spoon and spread them out on a clean dish towel or parchment (baking) paper.

Preheat the oven to 350°F/180°C/Gas Mark 4 and grease a large ovenproof dish with butter. Heat the béchamel sauce, add the Emmental, and stir until the cheese is melted. Remove from the heat and season with salt and pepper.

Place a layer of pasta in the bottom of the ovenproof dish, cover with half of the vegetables, then spread with one-third of the sauce. Repeat the layers, ending with a layer of bechamel. Bake for 20–25 minutes until golden. Serve hot.

LASAGNE AL RAGÙ, TARTUFO, E CREMA DI PORRI

LASAGNE WITH TRUFFLED VEAL AND LEEK SAUCE

AVERAGE

– Preparation time: *30 minutes*
– Cooking time: *1 hour*
– Calories per serving: *470*
– *Serves 4*

FOR THE LASAGNE

– butter, for greasing
– 1 quantity fresh Lasagne
  (see page 73)
– 4 tablespoons olive oil
– dry or toasted bread crumbs
– 12 oz/350 g ground
  (minced) veal
– 3 tablespoons dry white wine
– 1½ oz/40 g black truffle,
  ½ finely diced
– 2 eggs, lightly beaten
– ½ cup (1½ oz/40 g) grated
  Parmesan cheese
– pinch of freshly grated nutmeg
– salt

FOR THE SAUCE

– 3 tablespoons olive oil
– 3 leeks, trimmed and thinly
  sliced
– scant 1 cup (7 fl oz/200 ml)
  hot vegetable stock (broth)
– salt and pepper

Preheat the oven to 400°F/200°C/Gas Mark 6 and grease an ovenproof dish with butter.

For the filling, heat 3 tablespoons oil in a saucepan, add the veal, stir, season with salt, and cook for 3 minutes. Pour in the wine and cook until it has evaporated. Add the diced truffle, and cook for another 5–10 minutes. Take off the heat, let cool, then stir in the eggs, three-quarters of the Parmesan cheese, and the nutmeg.

For the leek sauce, heat the oil in a saucepan, add the leeks and 3 tablespoons water and cook for 5 minutes. Pour in the hot broth (stock) and cook for another 10 minutes. Season with salt and pepper. Remove from the heat, process in a blender, and return to the saucepan to keep hot.

Bring a large saucepan of salted water to a boil with 1 tablespoon oil, then add the pasta, a few noodles (sheets) at a time. When the noodles rise to the top of the pan, remove them with a slotted spoon and spread out on a clean dish towel or parchment (baking) paper. Cut each rectangle of pasta into 2 squares with a sharp knife.

Place 1 tablespoon of the filling in the center of each pasta square and fold it in half to form a triangle, pinching the edges to seal. Pour half the leek sauce into the oven dish and arrange the filled pasta triangles on top, cover with the remaining leek sauce, and sprinkle the surface with the remaining Parmesan cheese mixed with the bread crumbs. Bake for 20 minutes. Turn off the oven, take out the dish, grate the remaining half of the truffle over the surface, and return the dish to the oven for another 10 minutes.

CANNELLONI

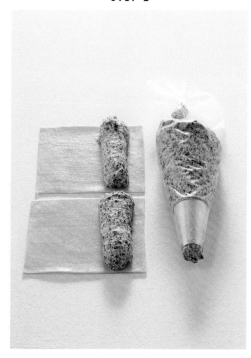

CANNELLONI ALLE ERBETTE
CHEESE AND SPINACH CANNELLONI

AVERAGE

– Preparation time: *30 minutes*
– Cooking time: *20 minutes*
– Calories per portion: *480*
– *Serves 4*

INGREDIENTS

– 1 quantity Fresh Egg Pasta
  (see page 17)
– 1 tablespoon oil
– 14 oz/400 g spinach leaves,
  finely chopped
– 1¾ cups (14 oz/400 g)
  sheep's milk ricotta cheese
– 1¼ cups (3½ oz/100 g)
  grated Parmesan cheese
– 1 egg, lightly beaten
– pinch of freshly grated
  nutmeg
– butter, for greasing
– scant 1 cup (7 fl oz/200 ml)
  light (single) cream
– salt

STEP 1
Preheat the oven to 350°F/180°C/Gas Mark 4. Roll out the pasta dough on a clean work surface into a thin sheet and cut it into 4-inch/10-cm squares (or use a pasta machine). Bring a large saucepan of salted water to a boil with 1 tablespoon oil, then add the pasta, a few noodles (sheets) at a time. When the noodles rise to the top of the pan, remove them with a slotted spoon and spread them out on a clean dish towel or parchment (baking) paper.

STEP 2
Combine the spinach and ricotta, then add half the Parmesan cheese, egg, a pinch of salt, and nutmeg. Spoon the mixture into a pastry (piping) bag fitted with a ¾-inch/1.5-cm nozzle (tip).

STEP 3
Pipe the filling along one side of each pasta square so that it forms an even ridge and roll up the pasta around the filling to form a neat cylinder.

STEP 4
Grease an ovenproof dish with butter and place the cannelloni in it, one by one, in a single layer. Pour over the cream, sprinkle with the remaining Parmesan, and bake for about 20 minutes, until golden and bubbling.

Tip: If you do not have a pastry bag, use a teaspoon to place the filling in the center of each pasta square, spreading it out to form a neat cylinder along the middle of each square. Carefully roll the pasta around the filling, enclosing it.

CANNELLONI ALLA BESCIAMELLA
CANNELLONI WITH BÉCHAMEL SAUCE

AVERAGE

– Preparation time: *40 minutes*
– Cooking time: *45 minutes*
– Calories per serving: *742*
– *Serves 4*

INGREDIENTS

– butter, for greasing and
  dotting
– 11 oz/300 g spinach
– 7 oz/200 g roast veal
– 1 slice ham
– ⅓ cup (1¼ oz/30 g) grated
  Parmesan cheese
– 1 egg, lightly beaten
– 1 tablespoon oil
– 1 quantity Fresh Egg Pasta
  (see page 17)
– 2 cups (16 fl oz/475 ml)
  Béchamel Sauce
  (see page 87)
– salt and pepper

Preheat the oven to 400°F/200°C/Gas Mark 6 and grease an ovenproof dish with butter. Roll out the pasta dough on a clean work surface into a thin sheet and cut it into 4-inch/10-cm squares.

Bring a large saucepan of water to a boil, add the spinach, and cook until wilted. Drain well and squeeze dry, then finely chop it. Grind or finely chop the veal and ham, then add the spinach, grated Parmesan cheese, and egg. Season with salt and pepper.

Bring a large saucepan of salted water to a boil with the oil, then add the pasta, a few noodles (sheets) at a time. When the noodles rise to the top of the pan, remove them with a slotted spoon and spread out on a clean dish towel or parchment (baking) paper.

Divide the filling and a little béchamel sauce among them and roll up carefully, without squeezing too much.

Lay the cannelloni, side by side, in the prepared dish, cover with the béchamel sauce and dot the surface with butter. Bake for 20 minutes. Let stand for 5 minutes before serving.

CANNELLONI DI FORMAGGI E VERDURE

CHEESE AND VEGETABLE CANNELLONI

AVERAGE

– Preparation time: *40 minutes*
– Cooking time: *1 hour
  30 minutes*
– Calories per serving: *483*
– *Serves 6*

INGREDIENTS

– 3 artichokes
– juice of 1 lemon
– 2 carrots, thinly sliced
– 2 zucchini (courgettes),
  thinly sliced
– 1⅓ cups (5½ oz/150 g)
  chopped green beans
– 3½ tablespoons (2 oz/50 g)
  butter, plus extra for greasing
– 1 leek, finely chopped
– 1 ripe tomato, cut into strips
– 7 oz/200 g stracchino cheese
– 1 cup (3 oz/80 g) grated
  Parmesan cheese
– 1 tablespoon oil
– 1 quantity Fresh Egg Pasta
  (see page 17)
– ½ cup peas (2½ oz/75 g)
– 2 cups (16 fl oz/475 ml)
  Béchamel Sauce
  (see page 87)
– salt and pepper

Trim the artichokes and cut them into sections. As you prepare the artichokes, discard the stem (stalk), outer leaves, sharp points, and central choke, and place them immediately in a bowl of cold water mixed with the juice of 1 lemon to stop them from turning black.

Bring a large saucepan of water to a boil, add the artichokes, carrots, zucchini (courgettes), and green beans and cook until almost tender, then drain well. Melt the butter in a skillet or frying pan, add the leek, and cook gently until softened. Add the boiled vegetables, season with salt and pepper, and cook for 20 minutes. Add the tomato and cook for another 2 minutes. Remove from the heat and allow to cool, then add the stracchino cheese and half the grated Parmesan cheese.

Preheat the oven to 350°F/180°C/Gas Mark 4 and grease 2 ovenproof dishes with butter. Roll out the pasta dough on a clean work surface into a thin sheet and cut it into 4-inch/10-cm squares. Bring a large saucepan of salted water to a boil with the oil, then add the pasta, a few noodles (sheets) at a time. When the noodles rise to the top of the pan, remove them with a slotted spoon and spread out on a clean dish towel or parchment (baking) paper.

Bring a saucepan of water to a boil, add the peas, and cook for 5 minutes, then drain. Return to the pan, add a small pat of butter in a small saucepan, and stir in the béchamel sauce.

Spread some béchamel sauce and cheese and vegetable mixture on each pasta square and roll it up. Arrange in the ovenproof dishes, pouring over the remaining béchamel sauce and grated Parmesan cheese. Bake for 20 minutes, then serve hot.

CANNELLONI DI CARNE E FUNGHI

MEAT AND MUSHROOM CANNELLONI

– Preparation time: *1 hour*
– Cooking time: *1 hour*
– Calories per serving: *1031–687*
– *Serves 4–6*

FOR THE CANNELLONI

– ¾ oz/20 g dried porcini
  (ceps)
– scant 1 cup (7 fl oz/200 ml)
  olive oil
– 1 carrot, finely chopped
– 1 stick celery, finely chopped
– 1 onion, finely chopped
– 3½ oz/100 g ground veal
– ½ skinless, boneless
  chicken breast, ground
– 4 oz/120 g chicken livers,
  chopped
– 1 quantity Fresh Egg Pasta
  (see page 17)
– scant ½ cup (3½ fl oz/95 ml)
  dry Marsala
– 2 eggs, lightly beaten
– ½ cup (1½ oz/40 g) grated
  Parmesan cheese
– pinch of grated nutmeg
– salt and pepper

FOR THE SAUCE

– 2 cups (16 fl oz/475 ml)
  Béchamel Sauce (see page
  87)
– 1¼ cups (11 oz/300 g)
  tomato puree (passata)
– ½ cup (1½ oz/40 g) grated
  Parmesan cheese

Soak the dried porcini (ceps) in a bowl of lukewarm water and set aside.

Heat the oil in a large saucepan, add the carrot, celery, and onion, and cook gently until lightly browned. Add the veal, chicken breast, chicken livers, and mushrooms, season with salt and pepper, cover, and cook over medium heat for 20 minutes. Preheat the oven to 350°F/180°C/Gas Mark 4.

Roll out the pasta dough on a clean work surface into a thin sheet and cut it into 4-inch/10-cm squares.

Pour in the Marsala, increase the heat, and let evaporate. Remove from the heat, put the mixture into a food processor, and pulse the ingredients. Transfer the mixture to a bowl and add the eggs, Parmesan cheese, and nutmeg. Check the seasoning and season with salt and pepper.

Bring a large saucepan of salted water to a boil, add the pasta, and cook for 2–3 minutes, or until al dente. Drain and spread out to dry on a clean dish towel. Divide the prepared filling among the pasta squares, then roll these up to make cylinders.

Spread a layer of béchamel sauce on the bottom of an ovenproof dish and lay the cannelloni on top. Pour over the tomato puree (passata), sprinkle with Parmesan cheese, and bake for about 30 minutes. Rest for 5 minutes before serving.

CANNELLONI DI ORTAGGI ALLA SORRENTINA
SORRENTO-STYLE VEGETABLE CANNELLONI

EASY

– Preparation time: *1 hour
+ 1 hour salting*
– Cooking time: *1 hour
20 minutes*
– Calories per serving: *395*
– *Serves 6*

INGREDIENTS

– butter, for greasing
– 1 large eggplant (aubergine)
– 2 red bell peppers
– 1 quantity Fresh Egg Pasta
(see page 17)
– 3 tablespoons oil
– 9 oz/250 g mozzarella cheese
– fresh basil leaves
– ⅔ cup (2 oz/50 g) grated
Parmesan or pecorino cheese
– scant 1 cup (7 fl oz/200 ml)
tomato puree (passata)
– salt and pepper

To prepare the eggplant (aubergine), cut them into
6 slices, put them into a colander, sprinkle with salt, place
a weight on top, and drain in a colander for 1 hour.

Preheat the oven to 400°F/200°C/Gas Mark 6 and grease
an ovenproof dish with butter. Roll out the pasta dough
on a clean work surface into a thin sheet and cut it into
4-inch/10-cm squares.

Roast the bell peppers in the oven for 30 minutes, turning
them halfway through the cooking time. Remove from
the oven and let cool, then skin and seed them, and cut
them into strips. Dry the roasted pepper strips on paper
towels. Turn the oven down to 350°F/180°C/Gas Mark 4.

Bring a large saucepan of salted water to a boil with
1 tablespoon of the oil, then add the pasta, a few noodles
(sheets) at a time. When the sheets rise to the top of the pan,
remove them with a slotted spoon and spread out on a clean
dish towel or parchment (baking) paper.

Cut the mozzarella cheese into strips and drain in
a colander, then dry them thoroughly. Pour 1 tablespoon
oil into an ovenproof dish, add the eggplant slices,
and sprinkle with the remaining 1 tablespoon oil. Bake
until golden on one side, then turn them over and brown
on the other side. Remove and set aside.

Divide the eggplant slices, roasted pepper strips,
mozzarella strips, and basil among the pasta squares.
Season with salt and pepper and sprinkle with grated
Parmesan or pecorino cheese. Roll up the cannelloni
and place in the prepared dish. Drizzle with the fresh
tomato puree (passata) and bake for about 20 minutes.
Remove and rest for 5–10 minutes before serving.

CANNELLONI ALLA NAPOLETANA
NEAPOLITAN CANNELLONI

AVERAGE

– Preparation time: *40 minutes*
– Cooking time: 1 hour
  5 minutes
– Calories per serving: *795*
– *Serves 4*

INGREDIENTS

– 3 tablespoons olive oil, plus
  extra for drizzling
– 3½ oz/100 g Italian sausages,
  casings removed and
  crumbled
– 12 oz/350 g ground (minced)
  beef
– 3 oz/80 g Neapolitan salami
  or pepperoni, skinned and
  chopped
– 2 eggs, hard-boiled and
  chopped
– butter, for greasing
– 1 quantity Fresh Egg Pasta
  (see page 17)
– ⅓ cup (1 oz/30 g) grated
  pecorino cheese
– salt and pepper

Heat 2 tablespoons oil in a large Dutch oven or casserole
dish and add the sausages, beef, and salami. Season
lightly with a little salt and pepper and cook gently
for 30 minutes over low heat, in batches if necessary,
until the mixture is fairly smooth. Remove from the heat
and add the hard-boiled eggs.

Preheat the oven to 350°F/180°C/Gas Mark 4 and grease
an ovenproof dish with butter. Roll out the pasta dough
on a clean work surface into a thin sheet and cut it into
4-inch/10-cm squares.

Bring a large saucepan of salted water to a boil with
the remaining 1 tablespoon oil, then add the pasta,
a few noodles (sheets) at a time. When the sheets rise
to the top of the pan, remove them with a slotted spoon
and spread out on a clean dish towel or parchment
(baking) paper. Divide three-quarters of the meat filling
over the cooked pasta squares and roll them up.

Arrange the cannelloni in the ovenproof dish and cover
with the reserved meat mixture. Sprinkle with
the pecorino cheese and drizzle over a little oil. Bake
for about 20 minutes. The top should spring back
when pressed pushed with a finger. Rest for 5 minutes,
then serve.

CANNELLONI ALLA CREMA DI RADICCHIO

RADICCHIO CANNELLONI

AVERAGE

– Preparation time: *40 minutes*
– Cooking time: *50 minutes*
– Calories per serving: *622*
– *Serves 4*

INGREDIENTS

– 3 tablespoons oil
– 3 tablespoons (1½ oz/40 g) butter, plus extra for greasing
– 1 shallot, finely chopped
– 5 oz/150 g ground (minced) chicken breast
– 3 heads radicchio, trimmed and finely chopped
– 1 quantity Fresh Egg Pasta (see page 17)
– 1 cup (8 fl oz/250 ml) Béchamel Sauce (see page 87)
– 5 oz/150 g fontina cheese, thinly sliced
– 2 tablespoons grated Parmesan cheese
– salt and pepper

Preheat the oven to 400°F/200°C/Gas Mark 6 and grease an ovenproof dish with butter. Roll out the pasta dough on a clean work surface into a thin sheet and cut it into 4-inch/10-cm squares.

Heat 2 tablespoons oil with a little butter in a skillet or frying pan, add the shallot, and cook until translucent. Add the ground (minced) chicken breast, stir, and season with salt and pepper. Sprinkle with 2 tablespoons hot water and cook gently for 5 minutes. Add the radicchio to the pan and cook for 10 minutes, increasing the heat, if necessary, to drive off any excess moisture.

Bring a large saucepan of salted water to a boil with the remaining 1 tablespoon oil, then add the pasta, a few noodles (sheets) at a time. When the noodles rise to the top of the pan, remove them with a slotted spoon and spread them on a clean dish towel or parchment (baking) paper.

Place a tablespoon of béchamel sauce on each pasta square and lay a thin slice of fontina cheese on top, followed by a little of the radicchio mixture, then roll them up.

Pour the remaining béchamel sauce into the prepared dish and arrange the cannelloni in it. Sprinkle with grated Parmesan cheese. Bake for about 20 minutes. Remove and rest for 5 minutes before serving.

CANNELLONI AI CARCIOFI
ARTICHOKE CANNELLONI

– Preparation time: *30 minutes*
– Cooking time: *55 minutes*
– Calories per serving: *740*
– *Serves 4*

INGREDIENTS

– 1 quantity Fresh Egg Pasta
  (see page 17)
– 3½ tablespoons (2 oz/50 g)
  butter, plus extra for
  greasing
– 1 small onion, finely
  chopped
– 1 clove garlic, finely chopped
– 6 artichokes, trimmed and
  chopped
– 2 tablespoons all-purpose
  (plain) flour
– pinch of freshly ground
  nutmeg
– scant 1 cup (7 fl oz/200 ml)
  vegetable broth (stock)
– 1 tablespoon finely chopped
  fresh flat-leaf parsley
– 1 egg, lightly beaten
– 1 cup (3 oz/80 g) grated
  Parmesan cheese
– 1 tablespoon oil
– 2 cups (16 fl oz/475 ml)
  Béchamel Sauce
  (see page 87)
– salt and pepper

Preheat the oven to 400°F/200°C/Gas Mark 6 and grease
an ovenproof dish with butter. Roll out the pasta dough
on a clean work surface into a thin sheet and cut
it into 4-inch/10-cm squares.

Gently melt the butter in a large, deep saucepan, add
the onion and garlic, and cook gently. Add the artichokes
and flour, stirring well, then season with a little nutmeg,
salt, and pepper. Pour the broth (stock) into the pan
and simmer for at least 20 minutes, then add the parsley
and process to a very thick puree using an immersion
(stick)blender. Add the egg, half the grated Parmesan
cheese, and a little béchamel sauce.

Bring a large saucepan of salted water to a boil with
the oil, then add the pasta, a few noodles (sheets) at a time.
When the noodles rise to the top of the pan, remove them
with a slotted spoon and spread out on a clean dish towel
or parchment (baking) paper.

Fill the squares with the artichoke mixture and roll them
up. Place the 12 filled pasta squares in the prepared dish.
Pour over the remaining béchamel sauce and sprinkle with
the grated Parmesan cheese. Bake for about 25 minutes.

---

*Tip: To make the garlic clove more digestible, peel it, cut it in
half, and get rid of the central green shoot before you chop it.*

CANNELLONI AI FRUTTI DI MARE
SEAFOOD CANNELLONI

ADVANCED

– Preparation time: *30 minutes + 30 minutes resting*
– Cooking time: *1 hour*
– Calories per serving: *370*
– *Serves 6–8*

INGREDIENTS

– about ¾ cup (6 fl oz/175 ml) extra virgin olive oil, for frying
– 1 shallot, finely chopped
– 14 oz/400 g cod fillet, thinly sliced
– 2 tablespoons white wine
– 11 oz/300 g raw shrimp (prawn) tails, thinly sliced
– 1 clove garlic, crushed
– 2 tablespoons brandy
– ¾ cup (7 oz/200 g) ricotta cheese
– 1 small bunch fresh flat-leaf parsley, chopped
– 2 egg yolks
– ⅓ cup (1½ oz/40 g) all-purpose (plain) flour
– 2 cups (16 fl oz/475 ml) hot fish broth (stock)
– ⅓ quantity Fresh Egg Pasta (see page 17)
– salt and freshly ground white pepper

Preheat the oven to 350°F/180°C/Gas Mark 4. Heat 4 tablespoons oil in a skillet or frying pan, add the shallot, and cook gently until softened. Add the cod slices and cook over low heat for 3–4 minutes, then season with salt and pepper. Pour over the white wine and let evaporate.

Heat 2 tablespoons of oil in a separate skillet or frying pan, add the shrimp (prawn) tails and garlic, and cook for 1–2 minutes. Pour in the brandy, evaporate, let it turn off the heat. Break up the cod with a fork and stir the fish into the ricotta with 1 tablespoon chopped parsley, the shrimp (prawn) tails, and the egg yolks.

Heat 4 tablespoons oil in a Dutch oven (casserole dish), add the flour, and cook for 2–3 minutes, stirring continuously. Trickle in the very hot stock and cook over low heat for 7–8 minutes, stirring continuously. Check the seasoning and add salt if necessary. Spread a thin layer of the sauce in an ovenproof dish measuring 8 x 8½ inches/20 x 22 cm.

Roll out the pasta dough on a clean work surface into a thin sheet and cut it into 4-inch/10-cm squares.

Bring a large saucepan of salted water to a boil with 1 tablespoon oil. Cook a few noodles of pasta at a time briefly, then drain them and lay out to dry on parchment (baking) paper. Fill each sheet with the fish mixture. Roll up the cannelloni and arrange them in the ovenproof dish. Coat them with the remaining sauce and bake in the oven for about 30 minutes.

RAVIOLI

STEP 1

STEP 2

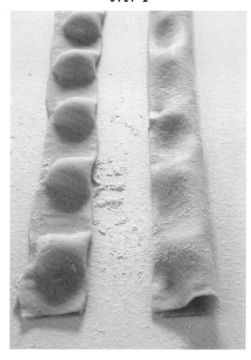

STEP 3

STEP 4

TECHNIQUE

RAVIOLI DI RICOTTA
RICOTTA RAVIOLI

INGREDIENTS

– 1¾ cups (14 oz/400 g) ricotta cheese
– 1¼ cups (3½ oz/100 g) grated Parmesan cheese
– 1 egg
– grated zest of ½ lemon
– pinch of freshly grated nutmeg
– ¾ quantity Fresh Egg Pasta (see page 17)
– 3½ tablespoons (2 oz/50 g) butter
– a few fresh sage leaves
– salt and pepper

STEP 1
Put the ricotta cheese into a bowl with the Parmesan cheese, egg, nutmeg, and lemon zest and season with salt and pepper. Stir well. Roll out the pasta dough on a clean work surface into a thin sheet (or use a pasta machine) and use a plain pasta wheel to cut it into strips 2½ inches/6 cm wide. Place teaspoons of the filling along one side of the strip, evenly spaced about 3 inches/7.5 cm apart.

STEP 2
When each strip is complete, fold over the pasta to enclose the filling and use your fingers to press all around it to seal, leaving no air pockets.

STEP 3
Cut the pasta between the mounds of filling with a sharp knife or a plain pastry wheel and spread them out on a lightly floured work surface while you finish preparing the rest.

STEP 4
Bring a large saucepan of salted water to a boil, add the ravioli, and cook for 3–4 minutes, or until al dente. Meanwhile, melt the butter in a small saucepan with the sage leaves. Drain the ravioli well, reserving some of the cooking water, transfer to a serving dish, and drizzle the melted butter and sage over them. If necessary, moisten the ravioli with 2 tablespoons of the reserved cooking water.

Tip: If the dough will not seal, brush a little water or beaten egg white along the edges before sealing the dough.

RAVIOLI

RAVIOLI DI MAGRO

CHEESE RAVIOLI

AVERAGE

– Preparation time: *30 minutes*
– Cooking time: *20 minutes*
– Calories per portion: *812*
– *Serves 4*

FOR THE RAVIOLI

– 12 oz/350 g semi-matured,
  semi-hard fontina cheese
– 2 tablespoons milk
– pinch of freshly grated
  nutmeg
– ⅓ cup (¾ oz/20 g) chopped
  fresh flat-leaf parsley
– ½ cup (2 oz/50 g) grated
  Parmesan cheese
– ¾ quantity Fresh Egg Pasta
  (see page 17)

FOR THE SAUCE

– 4 tablespoons (2 oz/60 g)
  butter
– 6 fresh sage leaves
– ⅔ cup (2 oz/50 g) grated
  Parmesan cheese
– salt and pepper

To make the filling, cut off the rind from the fontina cheese, dice it, and heat until softened in a heatproof bowl set over a saucepan of barely simmering water. Stir in the milk, adding a little at a time, and crushing the cheese dice with the bottom of a ladle or back of a wooden spoon until smooth and creamy. Add the nutmeg, parsley, and enough grated Parmesan for a soft but not at all liquid consistency.

Roll out the dough into thin sheets, divide it into strips, and cut it 2¼-inch/6-cm disks. Put a little filling in the center of the pasta disks, fold over the other half of the pasta sheet, and press the pasta down firmly around the mounds of filling to seal them.

To make the sauce, melt the butter over gentle heat with the sage leaves. Season with salt and pepper and keep warm.

Bring a large saucepan of salted water to a boil, add the ravioli, and cook for 3–4 minutes, or until al dente. Drain well and pour the sage-infused butter over them. Sprinkle with Parmesan and serve.

RAVIOLI DI RICOTTA CON ZUCCHINE E TIMO

RICOTTA RAVIOLI WITH ZUCCHINI AND THYME

EASY

- Preparation time: *15 minutes*
- Cooking time: *20 minutes*
- Calories per serving: *740*
- *Serves 4*

INGREDIENTS

- ⅓ stick (1½ oz/40 g) butter
- 2 zucchini (courgettes), diced
- 1 tablespoon chopped thyme leaves
- 3 tablespoons double (heavy) cream
- 1 quantity uncooked Ricotta Ravioli (see page 121)
- salt

Melt the butter gently in a saucepan over low heat without letting it brown, then add the zucchini (courgettes). Cook gently for a few minutes. Add the thyme, season with salt to taste, cover, and continue cooking for about 4–5 minutes. Pour in the cream, stir, and cook for another 2–3 minutes.

Bring a large saucepan of salted water to a boil, add the pasta, and cook for 3–4 minutes, or until al dente. Drain well and stir gently into the zucchini mixture to avoid damaging the ravioli. Transfer to a serving dish and serve.

Tip: You can vary the taste of this dish by adding 1 teaspoon finely chopped capers (rinse them well if they are preserved in salt) mixed with 1 teaspoon grated lemon zest.

RAVIOLI DI GALLINACCI AL TIMO

WILD MUSHROOM AND THYME RAVIOLI

AVERAGE

– Preparation time: *1 hour
   15 minutes* + *1 hour resting*
– Cooking time: *35 minutes*
– Calories per serving: *1,060*
– *Serves 2*

FOR THE PASTA

– 2⅓ cups plus 1 tablespoon
   (11 oz/300 g) all-purpose
   (plain) flour
– 1 egg plus 2 egg yolks
– olive oil
– salt

FOR THE FILLING

– 2 tablespoons olive oil
– 1 onion, finely chopped
– 1 clove garlic, finely
   chopped
– large pinch of fresh thyme
– 1 lb 2 oz/500 g wild
   mushrooms, cleaned and
   chopped
– ⅔ cup (2 oz/50 g) grated
   Parmesan cheese
– salt and pepper

FOR THE SAUCE

– 3½ tablespoons (2 oz/50 g)
   butter
– 1 tablespoon fresh thyme
– grated Parmesan cheese,
   to serve

Sift the flour into a mound on a clean work surface, make a well in the center, and add the whole eggs, egg yolks, oil, and a pinch of salt. Gradually combine them with the flour and knead to make a smooth, elastic dough. Wrap in plastic wrap (clingfilm) and let rest for 1 hour.

To make the filling, heat the oil in a saucepan, add the onion and garlic, and cook gently until softened. Add the thyme and mushrooms, season with a little salt, and cook for 20 minutes. Remove from the heat and let the mixture cool, then process it briefly in a food processor. Transfer to a bowl, stir in the grated Parmesan, and season with salt and pepper.

Roll the pasta dough out into a sheet and cut it out into 3–3¼-inch/8-cm squares. Brush the surface of each square with lightly beaten egg, place a little filling in the center, and fold in half, enclosing the filling. Pinch the edges to seal them.

Bring a large saucepan of salted water to a boil, add the pasta, and cook for 3–4 minutes, or until al dente. Drain well. Melt the butter in a saucepan and add the thyme leaves, then gently stir in the ravioli to coat with the butter. Serve with grated Parmesan cheese on the side.

RAVIOLI DI MELANZANE
AL BURRO
EGGPLANT AND TOMATO RAVIOLI

AVERAGE

– Preparation time: *1 hour
+ 30 minutes resting*
– Cooking time: *1 hour
15 minutes*
– Calories per portion: *450*
– *Serves 4*

FOR THE PASTA

– 2⅓ cups plus 1 tablespoon
(11 oz/300 g) all-purpose
(plain) flour
– 3 eggs
– salt

FOR THE FILLING

– 1 lb 2 oz/500 g eggplant
(aubergine)
– 2 tablespoons olive oil
– 3 tablespoons butter
– 1 onion, finely chopped
– 2 cloves garlic, finely
chopped
– 7 oz/200 g ripe tomatoes,
blanched, skinned, and
finely chopped
– fresh basil leaves, finely
chopped
– grated Parmesan cheese,
plus extra for sprinkling
– salt

Preheat the oven to 200°F/100°C/Gas Mark ¼. Slice
the eggplant (aubergine), place the slices in a colander,
sprinkle with salt, and let drain for 30 minutes. Rinse
the slices and bake for 30 minutes until dried. Peel off
the skin and chop the flesh finely.

Meanwhile, sift the flour into a mound on a clean
work surface, make a well in the center, and add
the eggs and a pinch of salt. Gradually combine them
with the flour and knead to make a smooth, elastic
dough. Wrap in plastic wrap (clingfilm) and let rest
for 30 minutes.

For the filling, heat the oil and 1 tablespoon butter in
a saucepan, add the onion and garlic, and cook gently
until softened. Add tomatoes and cook for 15 minutes.
Add the eggplant, cook, and reduce until the mixture is
thick and not too moist. Remove from the heat and stir
in the basil and grated Parmesan.

Roll out the pasta into a thin sheet. Place small, evenly
spaced mounds of the filling in rows along half the sheet,
then fold the other half over to cover the filling. Press
down around the filling to seal them, then cut them
out into ravioli.

Bring a large saucepan of salted water to a boil, add
the pasta, and cook for 3–4 minutes, or until al dente.
Drain well, then stir gently in a large skillet or frying
pan with the remaining butter and grated Parmesan.

*Tip: If fresh, flavorsome tomatoes are not available, try using
5–6 good-quality sun-dried tomatoes instead. Soak the dried
tomatoes in lukewarm water for 10 minutes before chopping
them finely and adding to the filling mixture.*

RAVIOLI ALLA MAGGIORANA
MARJORAM RAVIOLI

AVERAGE

– Preparation time: *1 hour + 30 minutes resting*
– Cooking time: *10 minutes*
– Calories per portion: *502*
– *Serves 6*

FOR THE PASTA

– scant 3 cups (12 oz/350 g) all-purpose (plain) flour
– 3 egg yolks
– 4 tablespoons dry white wine
– salt

FOR THE FILLING

– ¾ cup (7 oz/200 g) ricotta cheese
– 1 egg, lightly beaten
– ⅔ cup (2 oz/50 g) grated Parmesan cheese
– pinch of cinnamon
– 1⅔ cups (2 oz/50 g) chopped marjoram leaves
– salt and pepper

FOR THE SAUCE

– 7 tablespoons (3½ oz/100 g) butter
– ¼ cup (2 oz/50 g) superfine (caster) sugar
– ¾ oz/20 g marjoram leaves, finely chopped
– pinch of cinnamon

Sift the flour into a mound on a clean work surface, make a well in the center, and add the egg yolks, wine, and a pinch of salt. Gradually combine them with the flour and knead to make a smooth, elastic dough. Wrap in plastic wrap (clingfilm) and let rest for 30 minutes.

Combine all the filling ingredients in a bowl and chill in the refrigerator.

Roll out the pasta dough into a thin sheet and place small mounds of filling, evenly spaced out, on the pasta sheet. Fold over the other half of the pasta sheet and press the pasta down firmly around the mounds of filling. Cut out into ravioli and pinch the cut edges to seal them.

For the sauce, melt the butter gently in a saucepan and stir in the sugar and cinnamon.

Bring a large saucepan of salted water to a boil, add the pasta, and cook for 3–4 minutes, or until al dente. Drain well and add to the cinnamon-flavored buttery syrup. Remove from the heat, sprinkle with marjoram, and serve.

Tip: If you sprinkle a generous amount of pepper over the dressed ravioli, this will introduce a contrasting, pungent note to the sweetness of the sugar.

RAVIOLI DEL PLIN

PIEDMONT RAVIOLI

ADVANCED

– Preparation time: *20 minutes*
– Cooking time: *20 minutes*
– Calories per serving: *460*
– *Serves 4*

INGREDIENTS

– 9 oz/250 g escarole
– 1½ cups (7 oz /200 g)
  roasted meat, such as veal,
  rabbit and pork, plus any
  leftover jus (gravy), optional
– 2 eggs, lightly beaten
– 1 cup (3 oz/80 g) grated
  Parmesan cheese
– pinch of freshly grated
  nutmeg
– 1 oz/300 g Fresh Egg Pasta
  (see page 17)
– 3 tablespoons (1½ oz/40 g)
  butter
– fresh sage leaves, for
  garnishing
– salt

Trim the escarole and place it in a saucepan with just
the water still clinging to the leaves after rinsing it. Cook
for 5 minutes, until just wilted and tender. Let cool,
then squeeze it out carefully and chop finely. Finely chop
or grind (mince) the roasted meats and mix them with
the escarole, eggs, half the Parmesan cheese, a pinch
of salt, and a little grated nutmeg.

Roll out the pasta dough on a clean work surface
to a thin layer, then cut this into strips about 1½ inch/4 cm
thick with a ridged pastry cutter. Arrange evenly spaced
mounds of filling in the center of each strip until halfway
along the strip. Fold the empty half over the filling to make
the two layers of pasta stick to one another, then fold over
the pasta edge, placing the strip upright, with the filling
pointing upward.

Pinch the pasta between the filling mounds and cut out
the ravioli with a cutter. Bring a large saucepan of salted
water to a boil and cook the ravioli for 3–4 minutes,
or until al dente. Meanwhile, melt the butter with
the sage leaves. Drain the ravioli, then drizzle over
the melted butter flavored with sage leaves. Sprinkle
with the remaining Parmesan cheese or the leftover
jus (gravy) from the roasted meat.

*Tip: If the pasta dough seems dry and does not stick
together when you shape the ravioli, brush it with a few
drops of cold water.*

TORTELLI DI CARCIOFI E FORMAGGIO
ARTICHOKE AND CHEESE TORTELLI

AVERAGE

– Preparation time: *1 hour
20 minutes*
– Cooking time: *40 minutes*
– Calories per serving: *491*
– *Serves 6*

FOR THE TORTELLI

– ½ stick (2 oz/60 g) butter
– 6 baby artichokes
– 1 onion, thinly sliced
– ⅓ cup (1¼ oz/30 g)
all-purpose (plain) flour
– 2 cups (16 fl oz/475 ml) milk
– 3 eggs, lightly beaten
– ⅓ cup (1¼ oz/30 g) grated
Parmesan cheese
– 1 quantity Fresh Egg Pasta
(see page 17)
– salt

FOR THE SAUCE

– ⅓ stick (1½ oz/40 g) butter,
melted
– ½ cup (1½ oz/40 g) grated
Parmesan cheese

For the filling, melt half the butter in a saucepan, then add the artichokes, onion, and 2 tablespoons water. Cook gently for 20 minutes and remove from the heat. When the artichokes are very tender, chop them very finely.

Melt the other half of the butter in a small saucepan, add the flour, stirring quickly, and cook until it is a very pale golden brown. Gradually stir in the milk, adding a little at a time. Cook, stirring continuously, for 10 minutes. When the sauce is ready, mix it with the artichokes, off the heat, and stir in the eggs and Parmesan. Season with salt to taste.

Roll out the pasta thinly. Place a line of small mounds of filling on the pasta, leaving spaces between them. Fold the pasta sheet over them, press the pasta between the mounds, excluding any air, and cut between them. Pinch the edges together to seal. Continue until you have used up all the pasta and filling.

Bring a large pan of salted water to a boil, add the pasta, and cook for 3–4 minutes, or until al dente. Drain well and pour over the melted butter. Sprinkle with grated Parmesan to serve.

TORTELLI DI ZUCCA
PUMPKIN TORTELLI

ADVANCED

– Preparation time: *40 minutes + 2 hours chilling*
– Cooking time: *1 hour*
– Calories per serving: 875
– *Serves 6*

INGREDIENTS

– 2¼ lbs/1 kg pumpkin or butternut squash
– 2 cups (3½ oz/100 g) amaretti cookies (biscuits), finely ground
– 5 ½–7 oz/160–200 g mostarda di Mantova, chopped
– 2½ cups (7 oz/200 g) grated Parmesan cheese
– grated zest of 1 lemon
– pinch of freshly grated nutmeg
– 2 eggs, lightly beaten
– fresh bread crumbs, if needed
– ⅔ quantity Fresh Egg Pasta (see page 17)
– salt and pepper
– ⅓ stick (1½ oz/40 g) butter, melted, to serve
– grated Parmesan cheese, to serve

Preheat the oven to 350°F/180°C/Gas Mark 4. Put the pumpkin into an ovenproof dish, season with salt, cover, and bake for about 40 minutes, or until tender. Remove and transfer the pumpkin to a bowl and mash until very smooth. Add the amaretti, chopped mostarda, grated Parmesan, a little grated lemon zest, and the nutmeg, then stir in the beaten eggs, a little at a time, to make a firm filling. Season with salt and pepper. Mix well, cover, and chill in the refrigerator for 2 hours. When you take it out, the mixture should be firm; if not, add some bread crumbs.

Roll the pasta into a thin sheet. Using a pastry (piping) bag, pipe the filling into small, well-spaced heaps in rows on one half of the pasta sheet. Moisten the pasta all around the fillings.

Fold the other half of the dough on top of the fillings and press down between them, then cut out the tortelli with a fluted pastry cutter and pinch the edges to seal.

Bring a large saucepan of salted water to a boil, add the tortelli, a few at a time and cook for 3–4 minutes, or until al dente. Drain well and pour over plenty of melted butter and grated Parmesan to serve.

Tip: Mostarda di Mantova is a type of Italian candied fruit, combining candied fruits such as apples and pears in mustard syrup. It is available in specialty Italian grocery stores and online.

AGNOLOTTI ALLA PIEMONTESE

PIEDMONT-STYLE AGNOLOTTI

ADVANCED

– Preparation time: *1 hour*
– Cooking time: *2 hours*
– Calories per serving: *1,213*
– *Serves 6*

INGREDIENTS

– 1 tablespoon peanut
  (groundnut) oil
– 1¼ lb/500 g veal
– 14 oz/400 g pork
– 2 rabbit thighs
– 2 tablespoons olive oil
– 1 onion, chopped
– 1 clove garlic, crushed
– 2 cups (16 fl oz/475 ml)
  chicken broth (stock), heated
– scant ½ cup (3½ fl oz/100 ml)
  dry white wine, warmed
– 1 bay leaf
– 4 sage leaves
– 1 sprig rosemary
– 14 oz/400 g raw spinach
– 3¾ cups (11 oz/300 g)
  grated Parmesan cheese
– 3–4 eggs
– pinch of freshly grated
  nutmeg
– generous ¾ quantity Fresh
  Egg Pasta (see page 17)
– salt and pepper

Heat the peanut (groundnut) oil in a skillet or frying pan, add the veal, pork, and rabbit in batches, and cook until browned. Transfer the meat to a plate and set aside. In the same pan, heat the olive oil over medium-high heat, add the onion and garlic, and cook gently until the onions are softened. Add a little broth (stock), season with salt, and cook for 10–15 minutes. Add the meat, increase the heat, and pour in the wine. Tie together the bay leaf, sage, and rosemary to make a bouquet garni and add to the mixture. Season with salt and cook for 20 minutes. Add the hot broth (stock), cover, and braise for about 1 hour, or until the rabbit meat falls off the bone.

Let the meats cool in their juices, then bone the rabbit and finely chop all the meats. Discard the bouquet garni and garlic, add the spinach, and cook over low heat. Drain the spinach well and chop it. Put the meat and spinach into a bowl, add two-thirds of the Parmesan, and stir in the eggs. Season with salt, pepper, and nutmeg.

Roll out the pasta thinly and place mounds of filling in rows on it, leaving a generous margin between them. Fold the dough over the fillings and press down between them. Cut out the agnolotti into 1¼-inch/4-cm squares with a pastry wheel and pinch the edges to seal.

Bring a large saucepan of salted water to a boil, add the pasta, and cook for 3–4 minutes, or until al dente. Drain well, transfer to a serving dish, and drizzle over the hot meat juice and the remaining grated Parmesan.

TORTELLI DI RADICCHIO E ROBIOLA

RADICCHIO AND ROBIOLA TORTELLI

AVERAGE

– Preparation time: *30 minutes*
  + 1 hour resting
– Cooking time: *18 minutes*
– Calories per portion: *610*
– *Serves 4*

FOR THE PASTA

– 2½ cups (11 oz/300 g)
  all-purpose (plain) flour
– 2 eggs
– 2 tablespoons dry white wine
– salt

FOR THE FILLING

– 2 tablespoons olive oil
– 9 oz/250 g radicchio,
  finely shredded
– 7 oz/200 g robiola cheese
– ¼ cup (¾ oz/20 g) grated
  Parmesan cheese
– salt and pepper

FOR THE SAUCE

– 3 tablespoons (1½ oz/40 g)
  butter
– 1 teaspoon thyme leaves

Sift the flour into a mound on a clean work surface, make a well in the center, and add the eggs, wine, and a pinch of salt. Gradually combine them with the flour and knead to make a smooth, elastic dough. Wrap in plastic wrap (clingfilm) and let rest for 1 hour.

Heat the oil in a saucepan, add the radicchio strips, and cook until wilted. Season lightly with salt and set aside to cool. Stir the robiola cheese in a bowl until creamy and add a few tablespoons of grated Parmesan. Season with salt and pepper.

Roll out the pasta dough into a thin sheet and cut it into large disks, using a pastry cutter. Put a little filling in the center of each disk, then fold over, pressing down well around the edges to seal. Melt the butter gently with the thyme leaves and keep it warm.

Bring a large saucepan of salted water to a boil, add the pasta, and cook for 3–4 minutes, or until al dente. Drain the pasta well and dress with the butter and thyme. Serve hot.

RAVIOLI DI BRANZINO
SEA BASS RAVIOLI

AVERAGE

- Preparation time: *25 minutes*
  + 30 minutes resting
- Cooking time: *20 minutes*
- Calories per serving: *610*
- *Serves 4*

FOR THE PASTA

- scant 3 cups (12 oz/350 g)
  "oo" flour
- 1¼ cups (5 oz/150 g)
  semolina flour
- 3 eggs plus 4 egg yolks

FOR THE FILLING

- 2 (1 lb 8½ oz/700 g) sea
  bass, filleted, skinned,
  and boned
- olive oil, for cooking
- juice of 1 lemon
- 3 tablespoons (1½ oz/40 g)
  mascarpone cheese
- 1 tablespoon finely
  chopped chives
- salt and pepper

FOR THE SAUCE

- 6½ tablespoons
  (3¼ oz/90 g) butter
- fresh chives, coarsely
  chopped

Sift both types of flour into a mound in a large bowl
or on a clean work surface, make a well in the center,
and add the whole eggs and egg yolks. Gradually combine
them with the flour and knead to make a smooth, elastic
dough. Wrap in plastic wrap (clingfilm) and let rest
for 30 minutes.

Chop the sea bass fillets. Heat a little oil in a saucepan,
add the sea bass, and season with salt and pepper. Cook
for 10 minutes. Remove from the heat and let cool before
adding the lemon juice, mascarpone, and chives. Stir
very thoroughly.

Roll out the pasta dough into a thin sheet and distribute
small, evenly spaced mounds of filling along half of it.
Fold the other half over to cover it, pressing down around
the mounds to seal them and cutting between them
with a pastry cutter to make the ravioli.

Bring a large saucepan of salted water to a boil, add
the ravioli, and cook for 3–4 minutes, or until al dente.
Drain well and heat gently in a saucepan with the butter
and more chopped chives to serve.

AGNOLOTTI DI SPINACI
E BRASATO

SPINACH AND MEAT AGNOLOTTI

AVERAGE

– Preparation time: *40 minutes*
– Cooking time: *25 minutes*
– Calories per portion: *1,185*
– *Serves 4*

INGREDIENTS

– 9 oz/250 g spinach
– 3 cups (14 oz/400 g) braised
  meat, chopped and juices
  reserved
– 1 egg plus 2 egg yolks
– ½ cup (2 oz/50 g) grated
  Parmesan cheese, plus extra
  for sprinkling
– 5 oz/150 g ham, chopped
– 1 quantity Fresh Egg Pasta
  (see page 17)
– salt and pepper
– melted butter, to serve
  (optional)

To make the filling, bring a saucepan of water to a boil, add the spinach, and cook until wilted. Drain well, squeezing out any excess liquid. Chop it finely.

In a bowl, combine the spinach, braised meat, whole egg and egg yolks, whole egg, grated Parmesan cheese, and ham. Season with salt and pepper. If the mixture looks too dry, add a couple tablespoons of the braised meat juices.

Roll out the pasta dough on a clean work surface into a thin sheet and use a plain pasta wheel to cut it into strips 3 inches/7.5 cm wide. Place small mounds of filling, evenly spaced out, on the pasta sheet, fold over the other half of the pasta sheet, and press the pasta down firmly around the mounds of filling to seal them. Cut out square agnolotti with a fluted pastry wheel and pinch the edges to seal.

Bring a large saucepan of salted water to a boil, add the pasta, and cook for 3–4 minutes, or until al dente. Drain well and transfer to a serving dish. Sprinkle with Parmesan cheese and drizzle over the meat juices or melted butter. Serve.

AVERAGE

– Preparation time: *20 minutes*
– Cooking time: *8 minutes*
– Calories per serving: *475*
– *Serves 4*

FOR THE RAVIOLI

– 1½ cups (12 oz/350 g) ricotta cheese
– ¾ cup (2 oz/60 g) grated Parmesan cheese
– 2 pinches freshly grated nutmeg
– 1 egg
– 1 quantity Fresh Egg Pasta (see page 17)
– salt and pepper

FOR THE SAUCE

– 6 tablespoons (3 oz/80 g) butter
– 1 white truffle, cleaned, unsliced

Push the ricotta through a strainer (sieve) into a large bowl and mix with the grated Parmesan, nutmeg, and egg. Season with salt and pepper.

Roll out the pasta dough into a thin sheet and place small mounds of filling, evenly spaced in rows, along one half of it. Fold over the other half to cover them and press down between the fillings, then cut between the mounds to make ravioli, pinching the cut edges to seal them.

For the sauce, melt the butter over gentle heat. Bring a large saucepan of salted water to a boil, add the pasta, and cook for 3–4 minutes, or until al dente. Drain well and pour the butter over it, along with wafer-thin slices of truffle.

TORDELLI ALLA LUCCHESE
LUCCA-STYLE TORDELLI

AVERAGE

– Preparation time: *40 minutes*
– Cooking time: *30 minutes*
– Calories per portion: *790*
– *Serves 4*

FOR THE TORDELLI

– 2 tablespoons olive oil
– pinch of thyme leaves
– 5½ oz/150 g ground
  (minced) beef
– 5½ oz/150 g ground
  (minced) pork
– 2 oz/50 g mortadella,
  chopped
– 2 eggs
– ½ cup (1½ oz/40 g) grated
  Parmesan cheese
– ½ cup (1½ oz/40 g) grated
  pecorino cheese
– fresh bread crumbs, soaked
  in water and squeezed dry
– chopped fresh flat-leaf
  parsley
– pinch of freshly grated
  nutmeg
– 1½ quantity Fresh Egg Pasta
  (see page 17)
– salt and pepper

FOR THE SAUCE

– 3½ tablespoons (2 oz/50 g)
  butter
– fresh sage leaves

Heat the oil in a saucepan with a few thyme leaves
to flavor. Add the beef and pork and cook for about
10 minutes.

Remove from the heat and let cool. Mix the ground
(minced) meats, mortadella, eggs, 2 tablespoons grated
Parmesan, 1 tablespoon grated pecorino, the bread
crumbs, parsley, and nutmeg. Stir well and season with
salt and pepper.

Roll out the pasta dough into a thin sheet and cut out
3-inch/8-cm diameter disks. Put a small amount of filling
in the center of each disk, fold over the pasta, and seal
the edges. Melt the butter and sage leaves over low heat
and keep warm.

Bring a large saucepan of salted water to a boil, add
the pasta, and cook for 3–4 minutes, or until al dente.
Drain well and pour over the melted sage butter. Sprinkle
with the remaining grated pecorino and Parmesan
and serve.

RAVIOLI D'ANATRA
DUCK RAVIOLI

FOR THE RAVIOLI

– 2 duck breasts
– 2 duck legs
– 1 sprig fresh rosemary
– 2 fresh sage leaves
– 2 bay leaves
– 1 tablespoon butter
– 2 tablespoons olive oil
– brandy
– ½ cup (¾ oz/20 g) fresh
  bread crumbs
– 3½ oz/100 g prosciutto
  (Parma ham), chopped
– 1 egg, lightly beaten
– grated Parmesan cheese
– pinch of freshly grated
  nutmeg
– 1 quantity Fresh Egg Pasta
  (see page 17)
– salt and pepper

FOR THE SAUCE

– 1 tablespoon butter
– 4–6 tablespoons meat broth
  (stock)
– grated orange zest
– grated Parmesan cheese,
  to serve

Preheat the oven to 400°F/200°C/Gas Mark 6.

Place the duck in an ovenproof dish with the rosemary, sage, bay leaves, butter, and oil. Season with salt and pepper. Roast about 20 minutes, remove the breasts, and roast the legs for another 40 minutes, sprinkling it at intervals with a little brandy.

When the duck is well cooked, skim off the fat and reserve the cooking juices. Remove the skin, then remove the flesh from the bones and chop it finely. Place the meat in a bowl and mix with the bread crumbs, prosciutto (Parma ham), egg, grated Parmesan, and nutmeg. Stir thoroughly.

Roll out the pasta dough into a thin sheet and place small mounds of filling, evenly spaced out, on the pasta. Fold over the other half of the pasta sheet and press the pasta down firmly around the mounds of filling to seal them. Cut out into ravioli, using a 3-inch/7.5-cm round cutter, and pinch the edges closed.

In a large saucepan, add the butter and 1¼ cups (10 fl oz/300 ml) stock to the reserved cooking juices, stir in the grated orange zest, and heat through.

Bring a large saucepan of salted water to a boil, add the pasta, and cook for 3–4 minutes, or until al dente. Drain well and stir gently with the orange-flavored cooking juices, butter, and plenty of grated Parmesan cheese.

TORTELLINI

STEP 1

STEP 2

STEP 3

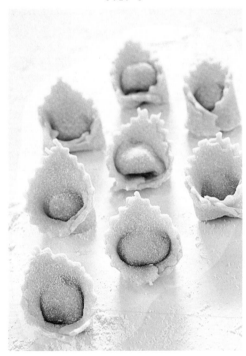

STEP 4

TECHNIQUE

TORTELLINI

TORTELLINI

ADVANCED

– Preparation time: *1 hour*
 + 30 minutes resting and
 24 hours chilling
– Cooking time: *40 minutes*
– Calories per portion: 450
– *Serves 4*

INGREDIENTS

– sprig of fresh rosemary
– 1 clove garlic
– 1½ tablespoons (¾ oz/20 g) butter
– 3½ oz/100 g pork tenderloin (fillet), diced
– 3½ oz/100 g prosciutto (Parma ham), finely chopped
– 3½ oz/100 g mortadella, finely chopped
– 1¼ cups (3½ oz/100 g) grated Parmesan cheese, plus extra to serve
– 1 quantity Fresh Egg Pasta (see page 17)
– pinch of freshly grated nutmeg
– 1 egg, lightly beaten
– hot beef broth (stock), to serve

STEP 1
Chop the rosemary leaves with the garlic and cook gently in the butter. Add the diced pork and a pinch of salt, cover, and cook over low heat for about 30 minutes. Drain the meat, let it cool, and finely chop. Combine the prosciutto (Parma ham), mortadella, pork, Parmesan cheese, nutmeg, and egg and mix well. Season with salt and pepper. Chill for 24 hours.

STEP 2
Roll out the egg pasta dough on a clean work surface into a thin sheet and use a fluted pastry wheel to cut out 1½-inch/4-cm squares. Place a small amount of filling in the center of each square.

STEP 3
Fold the pasta squares in half to form a triangle, seal the edges, and rest each one in turn on the pastry board with the longest side nearest you and the filled portion uppermost. Fold the longest side around your index finger so that the two opposite points of the triangle meet around your finger, brush the edges with egg, and press gently to seal.

STEP 4
Bring the beef broth (stock) to a boil in a large saucepan, add the tortellini, and cook for 2 minutes, or until al dente, then lift out with a slotted spoon. Serve in a soup bowl with plenty of grated Parmesan cheese on the side.

Tip: You can freeze any leftover tortellini. When ready to use, bring a pot of water to boil and cook the pasta for 2–3 minutes.

AVERAGE

– Preparation time: *40 minutes*
– Cooking time: *40 minutes*
– Calories per portion: *597*
– *Serves 10*

INGREDIENTS

– butter, for greasing
– 1 quantity Fresh
  Egg Pasta (see page 17)
– 5 oz /150 g ham, finely
  chopped
– 1 large cooked skinless and
  boneless chicken breast,
  finely chopped
– 1¼ cups (3½ oz/100 g)
  grated Parmesan cheese,
  plus extra for sprinkling
– ⅔ cup (5 fl oz/150 ml) heavy
  (double) cream, to taste
– chicken broth (stock),
  to serve
– salt and pepper

Roll out the egg pasta dough on a clean work surface into a thin sheet and cut out 4-inch/10-cm squares.

Put the chicken and ham into separate bowls and to each add an equal amount of grated Parmesan. Season with salt and pepper and combine with enough cream to make a mixture that is thick but not too firm.

Place an equal amount of chicken filling in the center of 10 pasta squares, cover each with a square of pasta, place an equal amount of ham filling on top of these second squares and cover with the remaining pasta squares. Use a round, fluted pastry cutter to cut out 10 tortelloni from the filled, layered pasta squares. Press the edges to seal.

Bring a large saucepan of salted water to a boil, add the tortellini, and cook for 4 minutes, or until al dente, then lift out with a slotted spoon.

Heat the chicken broth (stock). Serve the tortelloni with piping hot chicken stock and grated Parmesan on the side.

Tip: You can substitute the ordinary ham with the same quantity of smoked ham or prosciutto for a more intense but less delicate flavor. Reduce the amount of salt added to the filling accordingly.

TORTELLINI DI MAGRO
CHEESE TORTELLINI

AVERAGE

– Preparation time: *35 minutes*
– Cooking time: *20 minutes*
– Calories per serving: *421*
– *Serves 6*

INGREDIENTS

– 1½ cups (11 oz/300 g)
  ricotta cheese
– 2 eggs
– 1 cup (3½ oz/100 g) grated
  Parmesan cheese
– 1 teaspoon finely chopped
  fresh flat-leaf parsley
– 1 quantity Fresh Egg Pasta
  (see page 17)
– melted butter and fresh
  sage sauce (see page 123),
  optional
– salt and pepper

To make the filling, combine the ricotta cheese, eggs, Parmesan cheese, and parsley and mix well. Season with salt and pepper and let rest.

Roll out the pasta into a sheet and cut the pasta into 3-inch/7.5-cm disks. Place small mounds of filling on each disk, moisten the edges with your fingers dipped in water, and fold over to form a half-moon or triangle shape. The upper edge should stop fractionally short of the lower edge. Press the edges to seal.

Roll the filled pasta shapes around your index finger, pinching the two ends together tightly so they do not come apart when cooked. Place them on a clean dish towel that has been sprinkled with flour and let dry.

Bring a large saucepan of salted water to a boil, add the pasta, and cook for 4–5 minutes, or until al dente. Drain well and serve with melted butter and sage, if using.

Tip: When you seal the filling in the pasta, press down all around the filling, expelling any air so that the pasta pieces do not puff up when cooked.

CAPPELLETTI IN BRODO
CAPPELLETTI IN BROTH

AVERAGE

– Preparation time: *1 hour*
– Cooking time: *3 minutes*
– Calories per portion: *543*
– *Serves 6*

INGREDIENTS

– 1 cooked chicken breast,
  finely chopped
– 1 egg, lightly beaten, plus
  1 egg yolk
– ¾ cup (7 oz/200 g)
  ricotta cheese
– pinch freshly grated nutmeg
– 1 quantity Fresh Egg Pasta
  (see page 17)
– 6¼ cups (2½ pints/1.5 liters)
  beef or chicken broth (stock)
– grated Parmesan cheese,
  to serve
– salt and pepper

To make the filling, mix the chopped chicken breast with the lightly beaten whole egg. Beat the ricotta cheese with the egg yolk until it is creamy, combine the mixtures, season with nutmeg, salt, and pepper.

Roll out the pasta into a sheet and cut the pasta into 3-inch/7.5-cm disks. Place small mounds of filling, evenly spaced out, on the pasta sheet, fold over the other half of the pasta sheet, press the pasta down firmly around the mounds of filling. Bring the two ends together and pinch closed with your fingers.

Bring the broth (stock) to a boil in a large saucepan, add the pasta, in batches, and cook for 3 minutes, or until al dente. Serve with the broth, handing around grated Parmesan separately.

Tip: If you plan to serve these cappelletti in the traditional manner—in a beef or chicken broth—prepare the broth the day before, chill in the refrigerator, and remove all traces of the fat which will have solidified on the surface.

CAPPELLACCI DI ZUCCA
PUMPKIN CAPPELLACCI

AVERAGE

– Preparation time: *40 minutes*
– Cooking time: *30 minutes*
– Calories per serving: *1,115*
– *Serves 4*

INGREDIENTS

– 1¾ lb/800 g yellow-fleshed pumpkin, sliced
– 1 egg
– 1¼ cups (3½ oz/100 g) grated Parmesan cheese
– pinch of freshly grated nutmeg
– fresh bread crumbs, if needed
– 1 quantity Fresh Egg Pasta (see page 17)
– 6 tablespoons (3 oz/80 g) butter, melted
– salt and pepper

Preheat the oven to 400°F/200°C/Gas Mark 6.

Bake the pumpkin for 20 minutes, remove, and let cool slightly. Remove the skin and seeds and press the flesh through a strainer (sieve) into a bowl.

Mix the pumpkin flesh, egg, and ½ cup (1½ oz/40 g) grated Parmesan. Season with salt, pepper and a pinch of nutmeg. Stir well, and if the mixture is too soft, add a handful of bread crumbs.

Roll out the pasta dough and cut out 2½-inch/6-cm squares. Put a small amount of filling in the center and fold up the pasta into triangles, pinching the edges to seal. Bring the two lateral points together and pinch tightly.

Bring a large saucepan of salted water to a boil, add the pasta, and cook for 4–5 minutes, or until al dente. Drain well and dress with melted butter and remaining grated Parmesan cheese to serve.

Tip: If you want to use less butter when dressing the pasta, melt it in a saucepan, add a tablespoon of the pasta cooking liquid and stir to emulsify.

ANOLINI DI PARMA
PARMA-STYLE ANOLINI

AVERAGE

– Preparation time: *40 minutes*
– Cooking time: *2 hours
  40 minutes*
– Calories per serving: *828*
– *Serves 6*

INGREDIENTS

– 4 tablespoons (2 oz/60 g)
  butter
– 1 carrot, finely chopped
– 1 stick celery, finely chopped
– 1 small onion, studded with
  2 cloves
– 14 oz/400 g beef chuck
  (rump) steak, chopped
– 2 oz/50 g salami, skinned and
  chopped
– scant ½ cup (3½ fl oz/
  100 ml) red wine
– 1 tablespoon tomato paste
  (UK tomato puree)
– 1⅔ cups (14 fl oz/400 ml)
  hot beef broth (stock)
– 1 cup (1½ oz/40 g) fresh
  bread crumbs
– ⅔ cup (2 oz/50 g) grated
  Parmesan cheese, plus
  extra for serving
– ⅔ quantity Fresh Egg Pasta
  (see page 17)
– salt and pepper

To make the filling, melt the butter in a heavy saucepan, Dutch oven, or casserole dish, add the carrot, celery, and whole onion, and cook gently until browned. Add the beef and salami.

As soon as the beef is browned all over, add the wine, cook until it has evaporated, and season with salt and pepper. Stir the tomato paste (puree) into the hot broth (stock), add to the saucepan, cover, and cook for 2 hours over low heat, or until the meat is extremely tender and the cooking liquid greatly reduced. Remove from the heat and discard the onion and cloves. Strain the meat and vegetables, reserving the cooking liquid, then transfer to a food processor and pulse. Add the bread crumbs and grated Parmesan to make a filling.

Roll out the pasta dough into a thin sheet on a clean work surface and use a pastry wheel to cut it into strips 2½ inches/6 cm wide. Place teaspoons of the filling along one side of the strip, evenly spaced about 3 inches/7.5 cm apart. When each strip is complete, fold over the pasta to enclose the filling and use your fingers to press all around it to seal. Cut out the anolini with a round pastry cutter.

Heat the reserved cooking liquid in a saucepan and add a scant ½ cup (3½ oz/100 ml) water.

In a large saucepan, bring salted water to a boil, add the pasta, and cook for 4–5 minutes, or until al dente. Drain well, transfer to a bowl, and ladle the broth over the pasta. Serve sprinkled with Parmesan cheese.

FAGOTTINI DI ZUCCA
PUMPKIN FAGOTTINI

AVERAGE

– Preparation time: *40 minutes*
– Cooking time: *40 minutes*
– Calories per portion: *581*
– *Serves 3*

FOR THE FAGOTTINI

– 1 tablespoon olive oil
– 1¾ cups (7 oz/200 g) diced pumpkin flesh
– 2 small white onions or large scallions (spring onions, finely chopped
– generous 1 cup (9 oz/250 g) ricotta cheese
– 2 tablespoons golden raisins (sultanas), soaked and squeezed dry
– ¾ quantity Fresh Egg Pasta (see page 17)
– 16 whole chives, blanched
– salt

FOR THE SAUCE

– 2 tablespoons (1 oz/25 g) butter, plus extra for greasing
– 2 tablespoons all-purpose (plain) flour
– 2 cups (16 fl oz/475 ml) milk, warmed
– salt and pepper

Heat the olive oil in a skillet or frying pan, add the pumpkin, and cook for 15 minutes, until tender. Add the onions and season with salt and pepper. Beat the ricotta cheese in a large bowl with a wooden spoon and stir in the pumpkin and onion mixture, followed by the golden raisins (sultanas).

Preheat the oven to 350°F/180°C/Gas Mark 4 and generously grease an ovenproof dish with butter. Roll out the pasta into a sheet and cut it into eight 4-inch/10-cm squares.

Divide the filling into 8 equal portions and place one in the center of each pasta square. Gather up the corners of each square, enclosing the filling, and tie the neck of each little "bag" with chives, using two at a time. Bring a saucepan of salted water to a boil, add the bags, and cook for 2–3 minutes. Carefully remove them with a slotted spoon.

For the sauce, melt the butter, add the flour, stirring quickly, and gradually stir in the lukewarm milk in a thin stream. Cook, stirring continuously, for another 10 minutes. The resulting sauce should be of pouring consistency; add a little more milk, if necessary.

Put the pasta bundles in the prepared dish, pour the béchamel sauce over them, and bake for 5–10 minutes. Remove from the oven, stand for 5 minutes, then serve.

FAGOTTINI DI PUNTE D'ASPARAGI E FORMAGGI
ASPARAGUS AND CHEESE FAGOTTINI

EASY

- Preparation time: *25 minutes*
- Cooking time: *50 minutes*
- Calories per serving: *1,300*
- *Serves 2*

FOR THE FAGOTTINI

- ¾ quantity Fresh Egg Pasta (see page 17)
- 2 tablespoons (1¼ oz/30 g) butter, plus extra for greasing
- 1 onion, chopped
- 1 lb 5 oz/600 g asparagus tips, thinly sliced
- 3 oz/80 g fontina cheese, grated
- 6 oz/170 g Gorgonzola cheese
- salt

FOR THE SAUCE

- 1 cup (8 fl oz/250 ml) Béchamel Sauce (see page 87)
- 2 tablespoons (1¼ oz/30 g) butter

Preheat the oven to 350°F/180°C/Gas Mark 4 and grease an ovenproof dish with butter. Melt the butter in a skillet or frying pan, add the onion and asparagus, and cook gently for 15 minutes. Season with salt and remove from the heat. Combine the fontina and Gorgonzola in a heatproof bowl. Place over a large saucepan of gently boiling water and stir until both cheeses are melted. Add to the asparagus and stir well.

Cut the pasta sheet into 4-inch/10-cm-wide strips and cut these into squares.

Divide the asparagus and cheese filling among the squares and roll them up into little bundles or fagottini. Bring a large saucepan of salted water to a boil, add the bags, and cook for 2–3 minutes. Carefully remove them with a slotted spoon.

Arrange the fagottini in the prepared dish. Pour the béchamel sauce on top and dot with butter. Bake for 20 minutes.

PANSOTTI ALLA GENOVESE
GENOESE PANSOTTI

ADVANCED

– Preparation time: *30 minutes*
– Cooking time: *20 minutes*
– Calories per portion: *670*
– *Serves 4*

FOR THE PANSOTTI

– 1 lb/450 g borage, curly
  endive, or Swiss chard
  leaves
– ½ clove garlic
– scant 1 cup (7 oz/200 g)
  ricotta cheese
– 1 egg, lightly beaten
– 1¼ cups (3½ oz/100 g)
  grated Parmesan cheese
– ¾ quantity Fresh Egg Pasta
  (see page 17)
– salt

FOR THE SAUCE

– ½ cup (¾ oz/20 g) fresh
  bread crumbs
– ⅔ cup (5 oz/150 ml) milk
– 1 cup (5 oz/150 g) walnuts,
  toasted
– ½ clove garlic
– 3 tablespoons olive oil
– 1½ tablespoons (¾ oz/20 g)
  butter
– ½ cup (2 oz/50 g) grated
  Parmesan cheese
– salt

Soak the bread crumbs in the milk and set aside.

Bring a saucepan of salted water to a boil, add
the borage, and blanch until just tender. Drain well,
reserving the liquid, and chop it finely with the garlic,
then mix well with the ricotta cheese, eggs, and enough
grated cheese to make a thick mixture. Season with salt.

Roll out the pasta dough on a clean work surface into
a thin sheet and use a plain pastry wheel to cut it into
3-inch/ 7.5-cm squares. Place small mounds of filling,
evenly spaced out, on the pasta sheet, fold over the other
half of the pasta sheet, and press the pasta down firmly
around the mounds of filling to seal them.

To make the sauce, blanch the walnuts, remove their
thin skins, and pound them in a mortar with the garlic
and bread crumbs to form a paste. Gradually add enough
oil to make a pouring sauce, adding 1–2 tablespoons
of the borage cooking liquid to thin it, if needed.
Alternatively, place the walnuts, garlic, and bread crumbs
in a food processor and puree to make a coarse paste,
then stir in the oil. Season with salt.

Bring a large saucepan of salted water to a boil, add
the pasta, and cook for 2 minutes, or until al dente.
Drain well and add to the walnut sauce with a few
small pieces of butter and plenty of Parmesan cheese.
Stir and serve.

TORTELLINI DI CALAMARI
ALLA CREMA VERDE
TORTELLINI WITH PESTO AND SQUID

AVERAGE

– Preparation time: *35 minutes*
– Cooking time: *30 minutes*
– Calories per portion: *835*
– *Serves 4*

FOR THE TORTELLINI

– 4 cups (3½ oz/100 g) basil
  leaves, plus extra for garnish
– ⅔ cup (1½ oz/40 g) parsley,
  plus extra for garnish
– 2 tablespoons (¾ oz/20 g)
  pine nuts
– 1 tablespoon walnuts
– ½ cup (4 fl oz/120 ml)
  olive oil
– ¾ cup (7 oz/200 g)
  ricotta cheese
– 1 quantity Fresh Egg Pasta
  (see page 17)
– salt

FOR THE SAUCE

– 3 tablespoons olive oil, plus
  extra to serve
– 1 clove garlic
– 7 oz/200 g baby squid sacs,
  cleaned
– 2 tablespoons dry white
  wine
– 2 large, ripe tomatoes,
  skinned, seeded, and diced
– salt and pepper

To make the pesto, put the basil, parsley, pine nuts, walnuts, and olive oil into a food processor, process to a coarse puree, and transfer to a bowl. Add the ricotta cheese and salt and stir.

Roll out the dough into a thin sheet and arrange small, evenly spaced mounds of pesto in rows along one half of the sheet. Fold over the other half to cover and pinch the edges to seal. Cut out the tortellini with a round pastry cutter. Bring the two long points together and pinch to seal.

To make the sauce, heat 3 tablespoons oil in a skillet or frying pan, add the garlic and baby squid, then add the wine and let it evaporate. Cook for about 15 minutes. Remove the squid and cut them into thin rounds, then set aside.

Bring a large saucepan of salted water to a boil, add the pasta, and cook for 4–5 minutes, or until al dente. Drain well and transfer to the pan with the sauce. Discard the garlic, sprinkle with a little oil, and season with salt and pepper. Add the tomatoes and squid, chopped parsley and basil, and serve.

INDEX

Recipe Notes

Butter should always
be unsalted.

Eggs are assumed to be
extra-large (UK: large) size,
unless otherwise specified.

Milk is always whole, unless
otherwise specified.

Cooking and preparation
times are for guidance only,
as individual ovens vary.
If using a fan oven, follow
the manufacturer's instructions concerning
oven temperatures.

Some recipes include
raw or very lightly cooked
eggs. These should be
avoided particularly by
the elderly, infants, pregnant
women, convalescents,
and anyone with an impaired
immune system.

All spoon measurements
are level. 1 teaspoon = 5 ml;
1 tablespoon = 15 ml. Australian standard tablespoons are
20 ml, so Australian readers
are advised to use 3 teaspoons
in place of 1 tablespoon when
measuring small quantities.

Cup, metric, and imperial
measurements are given
throughout, and US equiva-
lents are given in brackets.
Follow one set of measurements, not a mixture, as they
are not interchangeable.

Phaidon Press Limited
Regent's Wharf
All Saints Street
London N1 9PA

Phaidon Press Inc.
65 Bleecker Street
New York, NY 10014

www.phaidon.com

First published 2015
© 2015 Phaidon Press Limited

ISBN: 978 0714 87002 1

Italian Cooking School Pasta originates from *Il cucchiaio d'argento estate*, first published in 2005; *Il cucchiaio d'argento cucina regionale*, first published in 2008; *Scuola di cucina pasta fresca e ripiena*, first published in 2013. © Editoriale Domus S.p.A. and Cucchiaio d'Argento S.r.l.

A CIP catalogue record for this book is available from the British Library.

Commissioning Editor: Emilia Terragni
Project Editor: Michelle Lo
Production Controller: Mandy Mackie
Designed by Atlas

Photography © Phaidon Press: Liz and Max Haarala Hamilton 6, 11, 22, 37, 41, 51, 57, 58, 61, 65, 69, 78, 81, 82, 86, 89, 90, 97, 103, 104, 111, 115, 124, 126, 128, 130, 135, 143, 144, 147, 148, 151, 157, 161, 162, 166, 169; Edward Park 42, 45, 54, 74, 110

Photography © Editoriale Domus S.p.A. and Cucchiaio d'Argento S.r.l.: Archivio Cucchiaio d'Argento s.r.l. 8, 13, 15, 16, 20, 25, 26, 29, 30, 33, 34, 38, 46, 49, 53, 62, 66, 72, 77, 85, 93, 94, 100, 107, 108, 112, 116, 120, 123, 132, 136, 139, 154, 158, 165, 170, 173

Printed in Romania

The publisher would like to thank Carmen Figini, Ellie Smith, Astrid Stavro, Nuria Cabrera, Lizzie Harris, Laura Gladwin, Theresa Bebbington, Susan Spaull, and Vanessa Bird for their contributions to the book.